About the Book

True Crime Astrology focuses an astrological lens on some of contemporary America's most famous homicides and suicide cases. Author Edna Rowland takes the reader deep inside the personality and motivations of the perpetrators and victims of the most irrevocable crime—the taking of a life.

This book, through its detailed analysis of people, events, and horoscopes, addresses the question that most people really want answered—WHY? What inner forces could bring people to lash out in such savage or cold-blooded vengeance? What part might victims unwittingly play in their own demise? How do people, events, and circumstances combine and result in such tragedy?

Prepare to enter a world of lives gone wrong, and lives lost too soon. *True Crime Astrology* is a fascinating look into the dark world of the killer, and the tragic fate of the victim. Rowland uses the tools of astrology to take the reader into the realm of the true detective—the story behind the crime.

"This attention-getting presentation just proves that there is nothing in the world that astrology cannot clarify."
—Doris Chase Doane, President
American Federation of Astrologers

About the Author

Edna Rowland is a professional astrologer, writer, and teacher. She lives with her husband John H. Rowland in Baton Rouge, Louisiana, where she has had a professional practice for over twenty years.

Her previous book, *Destined for Murder*, with co-author Sandra H. Young, was published in 1995 by Llewellyn Publications. *How to Obtain Your Birth Certificate: With Ready-To-Use Forms*, was published in 1990 by American Federation of Astrologers, Inc. She is a frequent contributor to many periodicals including *CAO Times*, *Dell's Horoscope*, *AFA Bulletin* and *American Astrology*.

Edna's credentials include professional-level certification through the American Federation of Astrologers, the New York Astrologer's Guild of America, and the California Church of Light. She is the recipient of the 1990 annual PAI award for her outstanding contribution to the art and science of astrology.

To Write to the Author

If you wish to contact the author or would like more information about this book, please write to the author in care of Llewellyn Worldwide, and we will forward your request. Both the author and publisher appreciate hearing from you and welcome your comments. Llewellyn Worldwide cannot guarantee a reply to all letters, but all will be forwarded. Please write to:

Edna Rowland
c/o Llewellyn Worldwide
P.O. Box 64383, Dept. K588–6, St. Paul, MN 55164-0383, U.S.A.

Please enclose a self-addressed, stamped envelope or $1.00 to cover costs.
If outside the U.S.A., enclose international postal reply coupon.

Free Catalog from Llewellyn

For more than ninety years Llewellyn has brought its readers knowledge in the fields of metaphysics and human potential. Learn about the newest books in spiritual guidance, natural healing, astrology, occult philosophy and more. Enjoy book reviews, New Age articles, a calendar of events, plus current advertised products and services. To get your free copy of Llewellyn's New Worlds, send your name and address to:

Llewellyn's New Worlds of Mind and Spirit
P.O. Box 64383, Dept. K588–6, St. Paul, MN 55164-0383, U.S.A.

True Crime Astrology

Famous Murders and Suicides

Edna Rowland

1996
Llewellyn Publications
St. Paul, MN 55164-0383, U.S.A.

FIRST EDITION
First Printing, 1996

Cover design: Tom Grewe
Page Layout: Kathy Thill
Project Manager: Ken Schubert
Photo Credits: All ©AP/Wide World Photos,
50 Rockefeller Plaza, NY, NY, 10020, U.S.A.

Astrology charts generated using WinStar by Matrix Software,
3115 Marion Avenue, Big Rapids, MI 49307, U.S.A.

Library of Congress Cataloging-in-Publication Data

Rowland, Edna.
    True crime astrology : famous murders and suicides / Edna Rowland.
    —1st ed.
        p. cm.
    Includes bibliographical references.
    ISBN 1-56718-588-6 (softbound)
    1. Astrology and crime.   2. Murder—Miscellanea. 3. Suicide—
    —Miscellanea. 1. Title.
    BF1729.C75R68 1996
    133.5'8364152—dc20   96-19695
                                                    CIP

Printed in the United States of America

Llewellyn Publications
A Division of Llewellyn Worldwide, Ltd.
P.O. Box 64383, St. Paul, MN 55164-0383, U.S.A.

Acknowledgements

The author is indebted to Julia A. Wagner of Dell's *Horoscope* magazine for permission to quote from and reprint the following article by Edna Rowland in book format:

"Suicide: The Last Choice." Reprinted by permission from *Horoscope* October, 1974. Dell Publishing Co., Inc.

I am also indebted to Kenneth Irving of *American Astrology* magazine for permission to reprint the following articles by Edna Rowland:

"Who Was the 'Fatal Vision' Murderer?" Reprinted by permission from *American Astrology*, November, 1986. American Astrology, Inc.

"Murder Unmasked—The Many Faces of Ted Bundy." Reprinted by permission from *American Astrology*, September 1987. American Astrology, Inc.

All of these articles have been revised and edited, and all other material in this book (with the exception of the above) is completely new and unpublished.

Other Books by the Author

How to Obtain Your Birth Certificate: With Ready-To-Use Forms
   (American Federation of Astrologers, Inc. CCS, 1990)

Destined for Murder: Profiles of Six Serial Killers
   (with Sandra Harrison Young, 1995)

Articles by the Author

"Suicide—The Last Choice" (1974)
   Dell Publishing Co., Inc./*Horoscope*

"Who Was the Fatal Vision Murderer?" (1986)
   American Astrology, Inc./*American Astrology*

"Murder Unmasked—The Many Faces of Ted Bundy" (1987)
   American Astrology, Inc./*American Astrology*

"O.J. and Nicole: An Astrological Profile" (1995)
   JBH Publishing Co./*Psychic Astrology Predictions: Annual Forecasts*

"The Moon and Crime" (1996)
   Llewellyn Publications/*Llewellyn's 1996 Moon Sign Book*

Table of Contents

Birth and death are not two different states, but they are different aspects of the same state.—M. Gandhi

Preface

Why pick a morbid subject like murder and crime to write about? I'll let my favorite true crime author, Colin Wilson, answer that question. In his new book, *Written in Blood*, the author says simply: "The problem of crime is the problem of human existence." I think that sums it up pretty well.

So, why did I write this book? My natal Ascendant ruler, Venus, is in Scorpio, the sign of the detective. The psychological motivation behind crimes of murder, and tragedies like suicide, has always intrigued me. As an adolescent, I preferred Sherlock Holmes mysteries to romance novels. Now, I am an avid reader of mysteries written by experts like Jack Olsen, Joe McGinniss, Shana Alexander, Ann Rule, Margaret Yorke, and others.

Being a Sagittarian, I'm supposed to be an eternal optimist, but I admit a Pollyanna approach to astrology simply doesn't work when describing or looking at violent crimes like murder or rape. In this book, however, I'm not describing bloody, gory crimes right out of *American Detective*, so you'll have to look elsewhere if that's what you want to read! All the crimes described here really happened, but as you've probably already guessed from the title, *True Crime Astrology: Famous Murders and Suicides*, this is a book about true crime with an accent on astrology.

Whether to sell more magazines, or just keep abreast of the current trends, most national astrology magazines, such as *American Astrology* and Dell's *Horoscope*, have already bravely ventured into the true crime arena. Articles of this type are flooding the market. Sun signs are "out" and true crime stories are "in." As a freelance writer, I've contributed feature stories on crime for both of these well-known astrology magazines.

Although at times I may sound somewhat like an amateur detective, my intention is not to catch criminals or make predictions. Rather, I'm attempting to look at some of the frequently overlooked "whys" and "wherefores" that often surround violent crimes. In most of the illustrated case histories collected here, the facts have already been reported and the criminals punished. The events have already occurred. As an astrology writer, I'm simply examining hidden or psychological motivations behind a few carefully selected crimes with the help of astrological techniques. However, the traditional journalistic who, what, where, when, and how of these stories have not been neglected.

This book contains a collection of true crime data on men and women who were motivated to kill. They have for one reason or another decided to break the commandment "Thou Shalt Not Kill." Many of these crimes were selected because they were so out-of-the-ordinary. I've tried to avoid being judgmental, and I'm not trying to change history. I'm just looking at crimes of violence from a different perspective: through the eyes of an astrologer. When the facts have been assembled and birth charts analyzed by astrology, further investigation may reveal hidden motivations that may or may not have been overlooked by our justice system in the process of bringing these criminals to trial, and hopefully, to conviction.

A few cases, like Marilyn Monroe's death, for example, tend to remain shrouded in mystery. Was her death suicide or murder? We may never know for sure, but it's intriguing to examine her birth chart, and some little-known events surrounding her death, in an attempt to look at facts from the astrological perspective. In analyzing or delineating charts of victims or criminals, I use transits and secondary progressions. I also occasionally employ some special techniques, such as prenatal eclipses and the prenatal epoch.

During the past twenty years of my career as a writer and professional astrologer, I've devoted many years of study and research to the subject of rape, murder, suicide, and accidents. I've tried to make the information presented here entertaining and informative to crime buffs and astrologers alike. For the sake of readers who may know little or nothing about astrological signs and symbols, I've included an introduction with some graphic tables. Readers already familiar with astrology may prefer to skip this introduction, but may, nevertheless, find the illustrated tables or keywords contained in the first chapter helpful for clarifying the particular meanings attributed to various planets and houses.

Astrologers will notice that I've placed special emphasis on the angles, especially the frequently neglected 4th house angle or cusp. Unfortunately, the 4th house angle has often been viewed or discarded as somewhat "taboo" because of the association with death and (horary) endings, but it is much too important to neglect.

I want to make it clear, however, that I view all the angles (the four angular houses and their cusps) as equally important. The angular houses are the 1st, 4th, 7th, and 10th. Most readers are probably already familiar with the Ascendant and Midheaven, terms astrologers use to refer to the cusps of the 1st and 10th houses. The terms "I.C." and "Descendant" may be less familiar; they refer to the 4th and 7th house cusps.

The "Cross" refers to the four-fold division of the circle or tropical zodiac into four seasons, four diurnal quadrants, four angles, etc. In general, the horizontal angles symbolize life, the vertical angles death. The cross is sometimes called the tree of life (and death).

Now that Michel Gauquelin's research in statistical analysis has refocused astrologers' attention on the importance of the angles (and their overlapping into cadent houses), most modern computer software programs offer aids for calculating Gauquelin sectors, which brings us to the big question of house systems; Which is the correct one? This is still a controversial question among astrologers. I prefer the Placidus house system, but I don't claim that it's the only valid system. One house system doesn't necessarily disprove another.

Nevertheless, all illustrated charts or horoscopes in this book are erected for the geocentric tropical or seasonal zodiac, and utilize Placidean houses. Wherever possible, sources of birth data have been cited. Although I use timed birth charts from birth certificates and have verified birth data wherever possible, some little-known rectification techniques have been employed where feasible. A brief explanation of these three rectification techniques for unknown birth times follows:

Prenatal Epoch: This rectification method should be used only when the birth time is known within one hour of accuracy, or the date of probable conception/ovulation is known. This method utilizes the horizontal angles of the natal chart (the Ascendant and Descendant). These angles exchange places with the Moon approximately nine months previous to birth, according to the Moon's phase at birth and whether it falls above or below the horizon. If E. H. Bailey's rules on the Prenatal Epoch are followed, there's also a gender factor to be considered, since the epoch may be either male or female.

The Moon, ruler of the fourth zodiacal sign, Cancer, rules motherhood and childbirth. The Moon's place at the epoch exchanges places with the natal Ascendant or Descendant. The resulting epoch chart can be progressed just like a natal chart. An example of this method of rectification (where the date of conception is known) can be found in Chapter 1.

Time-of-Death Formula: This is an an effective rectification method that can be used even if the birth time is completely unknown. However, this method can be used properly only when the time of death has been accurately recorded or a timed death certificate is available.

It has been observed that the angles of the death chart are often linked with, or interchange with, the signs or angles of the birth chart, especially the vertical angles. I haven't done lengthy or extensive statistical research on this phenomenon, but some examples are outlined here, and I've provided charts illustrating all four of the rules stated here. There are exceptions to the rules, but I feel that further research with a larger number of charts might prove rewarding.

Astrologer Jeannette Glenn, director of Western States Astrology Research Group (WSA), focused my attention on the concept of using the death chart for rectification purposes, and I gradually developed my own methods. As a registered nurse, Glenn has observed this angle-related phenomenon among dying patients, and although we agree on the basic importance of the death chart, we differ greatly in our methods of the application of these rules.

Utilizing this time-of-death formula for rectification purposes has one obvious disadvantage; namely, it can be used only _after_ the individual is deceased. For this study of murder and suicide victims, however, I was anxious to test it.

In a chapter on rectification in her book _Astrology: Old Theme, New Thoughts_, Joan McEvers illustrates her own version of this little-known time-of-death method with Ira Gershwin's birth and death. Natal or transiting Pluto is often found in or near one of the cusps of the angular houses in precisely timed death charts, as illustrated clearly in Gershwin's chart and by Ted Bundy's death chart in Chapter 5 of this book.

To use this method, a chart for transits at the time of death should be erected and compared to the natal chart. Although the exact formula for this exchange of angles is still being researched, some preliminary rules have been formulated. The natal 4th house angle or sign, signifying endings, frequently becomes the 1st house sign or Ascendant of the death chart when death is from natural causes and/or occurs close to the home. The Ascendant signifies the body and physical effects of death on the individual. Since most people die from natural causes or illness in old age, this is a common occurrence. (For example, see Dr.

Herman Tarnower's story in Chapter 7; he was killed in the bedroom of his own home.)

- The natal 4th house angle usually becomes the 10th house (public fame and fortune) sign on the angle of the death chart when death is by homicide or public execution. The death of a notorious criminal or famous person is often announced by the media, accompanied by extensive publicity. (For example, see Ted Bundy's precisely timed execution chart in Chapter 5).

- When the natal 4th house angle interchanges with the public 7th house angle of the death chart, a spouse or business partner may be involved in the death. The 7th is a public, not private, house, so death can be by assassination by public or open enemies, or homicide. (For example, see Marilyn Monroe's death in Chapter 9.)

- When an individual commits suicide, the signs and cusps of the death chart may closely resemble the birth chart pattern or "repeat" the natal angles (almost to the degree). Since suicide usually requires a certain amount of secrecy, the 4th house cusp (a private matter) appears to remain fixed in time. There may also be significant progressed aspects to the ruler of the 12th house of secrets, and its occupants. Close duplication of the natal Ascendant sign in the event chart of death—the mirror effect—usually indicates that death was self-inflicted. Those who believe in reincarnation, or karma, may speculate as to whether this suggests that the individual may be required to repeat this incarnation. (For example, Sylvia Plath's suicide; see Chapter 10).

Rectification by Events: Last, but not least, I've used this traditional and reliable rectification method of checking a natal chart by looking at several important events such as marriage, divorce, surgery, a parent's death, etc. For example, Marilyn Monroe's chart has been carefully checked by transits and secondary progressions to her natal chart for three consecutive events—her three marriages. Before acceptance, all rectified or speculative birth charts (and epoch charts as well) should be required to pass this final test.

The exchange of angles and their duplication at the time of birth or death may have been going on under our noses for a long, long time. It's not a new phenomenon, but as astrologers, our obsession with planets and their zodiacal sign positions may have obscured our vision.

Until we examine this phenomenon more closely, we shouldn't discard the houses or diminish their significance. Instead, perhaps we should take a much closer look at them. There may still be much to learn by exploring new methods and extending our perspective.

Edna Rowland
Baton Rouge, LA

An Introduction to Astrology

U ranus rules astrology. It is the planet that has been assigned to astrologers. It also rules the principle of individuation—the drive to attain the freedom to be oneself. Sometimes freedom can be attained only by revolution. Uranus is a rebel.

Uranus takes about eighty-four years to move through its orbit. It was in Aquarius, its native sign, from 1912 until 1919. At that time, interest in astrology greatly increased. In the United States, Evangeline Adams became a popular astrological speaker and consultant. In England, Alan Leo brought the subject to the attention of the public with his books and publications. This transit repeats itself from 1996 until 2003, and the three Uranus/Neptune conjunctions in 1993 helped to prepare us for this event by gradually accelerating our evolutionary pace.

Due to the precession of the equinoxes, we are now in a stage of transition between the ages of Pisces and Aquarius. Neptune, ruler of Pisces, and Uranus, ruler of Aquarius, must meet and pave the way for the coming New Age which is almost upon us. Computers have already revolutionized the way astrologers approach their trade. Computers are ruled by Uranus (electricity) as well as by Mercury. Now that astrology software is readily available, few astrologers erect charts by hand any longer. Research on astrological techniques has also speeded up and astrologers now have access to large data banks and electronic bulletin boards. As a result, astrologers, as a group, are generally becoming more professional and more research-oriented than ever before.

Astrologers measure cycles between birth and death by different methods or techniques. *Transits* and *progressions* to natal planets are the usual methods of measurement, although they are by no means the only ones.

Using the transit method, the positions of the Sun, Moon, and planets on a particular day and time are noted and compared to their positions at the moment of an individual's birth. Transits tend to be more environmental than individualistic, since they apply to everyone.

In contrast, progressions are like the unfolding, or growth, in slow motion, of the inherent potentials or characteristics of an individual. The *secondary progression*, which I use throughout this book, is one of the most popular systems used by modern astrologers to plot events and map psychological development. Progressions are closely tied to the individual's age and designate their inner growth or development. This method utilizes a simple formula called *a day for a year*. Each day after birth is equivalent to one year in that individual's life. For instance, to do a progression for a twenty-year-old person, the astrologer would cast a chart for twenty days after the date of birth. The positions of the progressed planets on that date, and aspects to natal planets, symbolize conditions that will most likely be met during the particular time in question. Using this method, past events as well as future events can be viewed while using the natal chart as a constant or fixed present factor. I use the Sun's longitude (or solar arc) to progress the MC. With this simple method, the Sun's natal longitude is subtracted from the Sun's progressed longitude, and the sum is then added to the natal MC.

As our awareness or consciousness expands and grows, so can we decide of our own free will either to fully participate in the objective universe around us or withdraw into the security of our own subjective inner world. In astrology, this is symbolized by the fixed horizon line that divides the horoscope into two parts—upper and lower, or day and night. This horizon defines the boundary between our public and private lives.

Astrology affirms and confirms the continuing relationship of the Earth to the other eight planets, as well as to the Sun and Moon. Astrology acknowledges, or attempts to prove, the ongoing relationship between planets and human beings. Astronomy, while painstakingly measuring and recording planetary positions and the planets' changing patterns or orbits, continues to deny any relationship or observed effects between planetary motions and human behavior.

Understanding the Signs of the Zodiac

Keeping these differences in mind, let's examine some of the precepts and principles of tropical or geocentric astrology.

The ecliptic is the Sun's apparent path around the Earth. This circle of 360 degrees is called the zodiac and is divided into segments (signs) of 30 degrees each. This is called the seasonal or Tropical Zodiac, which begins with 0° Aries, corresponding to the first day of Spring.

Aries, Taurus, and Gemini are the Spring signs; Cancer, Leo, and Virgo are the Summer signs; Libra, Scorpio, and Sagittarius are the Fall signs; and Capricorn, Aquarius, and Pisces, the Winter signs. This is the order of the signs and seasons in the northern hemisphere; the order is reversed in the southern hemisphere, where the first day of Spring occurs at 0° Libra.

Table 1 provides the names and symbols of the signs of the zodiac, as

Table 1: Signs, Symbols, and Keywords

	Signs	Symbols	Planetary Keywords	Ruling Planets	Symbols
1.	Aries	♈	Action Aggression	Mars	♂
2.	Taurus	♉	Love Pleasure	Venus/ Transpluto	♀ ♟
3.	Gemini	♊	Mind Communication	Mercury	☿
4.	Cancer	♋	Feelings Instincts	Moon	☽
5.	Leo	♌	Consciousness Ego	Sun	☉
6.	Virgo	♍	Mind Analysis	Mercury	☿
7.	Libra	♎	Love Artistry	Venus	♀
8.	Scorpio	♏	Aggression Transformation	Mars/ Pluto	♂ ♇
9.	Sagittarius	♐	Growth Expansion	Jupiter	♃
10.	Capricorn	♑	Authority Restriction	Saturn	♄
11.	Aquarius	♒	Authority Freedom	Saturn/ Uranus	♄ ♅
12.	Pisces	♓	Expansion Sacrifice	Jupiter/ Neptune	♃ ♆

well as the names and symbols of the planets that rule each sign (ruling planets). Note that some signs have more than one ruler.

In addition to the traditional planetary symbols listed in Table 1, other symbols are also used in this book. For example, the asteroid Chiron, discovered between the orbits of Saturn and Uranus, is indicated by the symbol (⚷), and the hypothetical, undiscovered planet, Transpluto, also known as Bacchus, by the symbol (♇). Other sensitive points referred to in this book are the Vertex (Vx), the Anti-Vertex (Ax), the Equatorial Ascendant or East Point (EP), and the Prenatal Eclipse (PE).

Eclipses and Why They Are So Important

The Moon's Nodes are two points opposite each other where the Moon crosses the ecliptic. These two points are called the North Node (☊) and the South Node (☋). Whenever the Earth, Moon, and Sun are transiting close to the Moon's Nodes, an eclipse can occur; therefore, these are sensitive points in the horoscope. Considered as an astronomical event, an eclipse is temporary, lasting only a short time; however, astrologically its effects may last for years or even decades. Most astrologers agree that the effects of a solar eclipse last *longer* than a lunar eclipse, probably about one year. Solar eclipses can occur only at a New Moon.

A prenatal eclipse (PE) is a solar eclipse occurring *before* birth; this is a sensitive point and, according to Rose Lineman in her book *Your Prenatal Eclipse*, denotes the karma of past relationships.

The nodes, which move backward through the zodiac, complete their cycle approximately every eighteen to nineteen years, and it is at this time that the Sun, Moon, and lunar nodes repeat their same relative positions. Eclipses that occur following the completion of a nodal cycle tend to repeat themselves in nearly the same order.

Revolutions, wars, and other types of disasters tend to occur whenever planets cross important "sensitive points" in recent eclipse charts. Take, for example, the beginning of the war with Iraq in 1991. President Bush made the announcement about the war on television at 7:00 P.M. EST from Washington, D.C. on January 16, 1991. An annual solar eclipse (New Moon at 25° 20' Capricorn) took place just twenty-four hours earlier, on January 15, 1991, at 6:50 P.M. EST. On July 20, 1963, an eclipse fell on President John F. Kennedy's natal 4th house ruler, Saturn, at 27° Cancer; he was assassinated on November 20, 1963, when the transiting Sun was at 27° Scorpio.

Understanding the Twelve Houses

The zodiac is divided into twelve segments called *houses*, with the boundary line of each house called the *cusp*. The 4th house cusp, at the bottom of a chart, is the Midnight point, marking the beginning and ending of the day. The degrees of longitude on the opposite 10th house cusp, or Midheaven, change approximately every four minutes, making one complete cycle through the 360 degrees of the zodiac every day.

The Ascendant, or rising sign, on the 1st house cusp, is determined by the time of birth as well as by the latitude and longitude of the birthplace. To calculate a natal chart or horoscope for an individual and determine the exact positions of the planets, an astrologer must know the correct time and date of birth, and the birthplace. Capricorn, Aquarius, Pisces, Aries, Taurus, and Gemini are known as the signs of short ascension. They move fastest through the Ascendant, but a new sign passes through the Midheaven or MC approximately every two hours. This is why the time is such an important factor in determining the exact degree of the rising sign or Ascendant. Signs move through the houses, not vice versa; the houses are constant and do not move. In contrast to the signs, which describe innate characteristics of human personality, houses denote different departments of life and govern outer circumstances or environment.

Table 2 provides a general guide to the departments of life that each house rules or governs.

The Planets—What They Mean

Aside from the Earth, there are eight known planets, in addition to the Sun and Moon (luminaries), which traverse or transit the zodiacal signs and houses, resulting in changing circumstances as they aspect, or come in contact with, the natal planets. The planets are Mercury, Venus, Mars, Jupiter, Saturn, Uranus, Neptune, and Pluto. For convenience, astrologers often refer to the Sun and Moon as "planets," although it is understood

Table 2: The Influence of the Houses

House	Departments of Life
1st	Outer personality; physical body; personal appearance.
2nd	Finances; your earnings and values; other people's death.
3rd	Siblings; neighbors; short term travel; early schooling or education.
4th	Home; heritage; the father (in female chart); the mother (in male chart); old age; end of life.
5th	Children; love affairs; creativity; speculation; gambling.
6th	Health; diet; employment; co-workers; military service; servants.
7th	Marriage or business partners; litigation and legal judgments; open enemies; public opinion.
8th	Death; inheritance; insurance; major surgery; sex; taxes; other people's money.
9th	Religious beliefs and ethics; legalities; higher education (college); publishing; long trips.
10th	Profession; your employer or boss; fame; reputation; the mother (female chart); the father (male chart).
11th	Friendships; clubs and group activities; adoption; hopes and wishes; the partner's children (step-children).
12th	Secret enemies; family secrets; the past before birth; hospitalization or imprisonment; hidden addictions and vices; self-undoing or self-destruction (suicide).

by all that the Moon is a satellite and the Sun is a star. Uranus, Neptune, and Pluto are often referred to as "outer" planets because of their distance from the Sun, and the fact that they move so slowly. The other five planets are called inner planets.

Planets are classified according to their speed or motion. Some of them, like the Moon, traverse the entire zodiac within one month, whereas the Sun completes the round of the zodiac within one year. The outer planet Uranus takes about seven years to travel throughout one sign, whereas the inner planet Jupiter requires only one year to traverse a single sign. Their influences differ not only because of speed, but because of the planet's assigned rulership of certain signs, and planetary placements in individual horoscopes. Astrologers assign certain characteristics, or meanings, to each planet, commonly called "keywords," and may divide planets into classifications such as masculine or feminine. Planets also have certain dignities and debilities, or strengths and weaknesses, according to their placement in particular signs or houses.

When interpreting a natal chart, the Ascendant sign ruler, or chart ruler, as well as the Sun and Moon sign ruler(s), are usually given greater importance or emphasis. Angular planets, and those forming a "stellium" (three or more planets within the same sign or house), are also given dominant status; angular planets are those occupying the 1st, 4th, 7th, and 10th houses. A culminating planet is a planet reaching the highest point in the sky, and usually refers to a planet residing within the 10th house, or near the cusp of the Midheaven (MC).

Understanding the Aspects Between Planets

Aspects, or relationships between the planets, also determine the influence of the planets. Analysis of a chart depends to a great extent on the study of aspects, or the distance between two planets as measured by degrees of longitude. Orbs are allowed, so aspects need not be exact. An average five- to eight-degree orb is allowed for natal aspects, but sometimes as much as ten degrees is allowed for aspects involving the Sun or Moon. Some aspects, such as the semisextile, inconjunct, semisquare, or sesquiquadrate, require a much smaller orb.

Contemporary astrologers tend to differ on the subject of allowed orbs, but most astrologers generally agree that *progressed* aspects require a small orb of only one degree on either side of an exact aspect. Aspects may be either applying or separating from a particular degree, but exact or applying aspects are usually given more importance. Table 3 lists the most

Table 3: Orbs of Aspects

Aspects	Distance in Longitude	Orbs
Conjunction	0° Longitude	10-12°
Semisextile	30° Longitude	1-2°
Semisquare	45° Longitude	2-4°
Sextile	60° Longitude	7-8°
Square	90° Longitude	7-8°
Trine	120° Longitude	7-8°
Sesquiquadrate	135° Longitude	2-4°
Inconjunct	150° Longitude	2-4°
Opposition	180° Longitude	7-8°
Parallel	0° Declination	0-1°

Orbs: 8° orb allowed for transits/natal; 10° for conjunctions, and 12° for aspects involving the Sun or Moon. But allow only 1° orb applying or separating for all progressions.

commonly used aspects with their customary orbs.

Some aspects are called *soft* aspects. These are the trines (120°), sextiles (60°), semisextiles (30°), and conjunctions (0°) of benefic planets like Venus and Jupiter. Conjunctions between malefic planets like Mars and Saturn, for instance, and aspects such as oppositions (180°), squares (90°), semisquares (45°), and sesquiquadrates (135°) are *hard* aspects. *Affliction* is a commonly used term to denote a planet or midpoint that receives difficult or hard aspects from other planets, especially malefics, or is in conjunction with malefics. The term "affliction" is used by astrologers mainly for convenience in describing patterns, midpoints, or aspects denoting particularly stressful or troublesome areas in a chart. However, no chart is good or bad just because it contains a surplus of predominantly *soft* or *hard* aspects. The whole chart must be examined carefully in its entirety before making judgments. Whether the chart belongs to a male or female must also be considered, as must the person's age, and environmental or genetic factors. Most charts contain a large number of *both* types of aspects.

One possible effect of a large number of hard aspects is to make a person overly aggressive or even violent, especially when the individual fails to channel the inevitable stresses. In some cases, they may only result in a workaholic or an overly ambitious individual who may be troubled with ulcers, depression, or other symptoms of prolonged stress. Positive individuals who learn to handle stress and sublimate their negative emotions may attain success by rising to the challenge of their hard aspects. A stressful T–Cross or Grand Square pattern may even bestow the necessary drive to succeed where others have failed.

The rare chart without any hard aspects may belong to a person who has never learned to meet challenges. This person could eventually become too dependent or passive to cope with the daily problems of life. Thus, although soft aspects are considered less stressful and more harmonious, a chart with too many soft aspects may be the signature of a person who is passive, weak, or simply lazy and permissive. Maybe this is why the ancients considered the Grand Trine an affliction rather than a blessing.

Although contemporary astrologers feel that favorable soft aspects allow a greater probability of integration, most will agree that hard aspects are often needed to activate a person into overcoming personal problems or conditioning, and improving environmental conditions. "No pain, no gain," as the saying goes. Again, everything depends on the individual and how he or she learns to meet and overcome challenges, or compensate for them. Thus, the ideal chart is one with a balanced combination of both soft and hard aspects.

Aspects represent the potential energies available to an individual, which may be utilized positively or negatively according to the person's free will and ability to make proper choices. Some individuals succeed despite formidable obstacles. I've observed that criminals, and those in law enforcement occupations such as police officers and detectives, frequently have similar aspects, but obviously they tend to use these energies differently. As can be expected, the masculine, violent planets Mars and Pluto are often accented; private detectives and spies, on the other hand, often have the feminine ESP planet Neptune heavily aspected or in the 12th house. For example, Stephen King, the horror writer, has a harsh Saturn/Pluto conjunction in his 1st house that trines his MC.

Individuals vary greatly in their abilities and talents. It's to be expected that while some predominantly Cardinal sign individuals may make an effort to change or overcome a difficult environment, Mutable sign individuals may prefer to adjust to the environment, or leave it, rather than make an effort to change it, while Fixed sign people most often dig in and rely on the power of persistence, as they tend to make the most of the situation at hand.

However, our modern world does give individuals more choices and offer more mobility. No doubt this is one reason relocational astrology has become an increasingly popular technique, since it recognizes the fact that the birthplace is no longer an absolutely fixed factor in the art of horoscopy. Our ancestors often lived and died close to their birthplace, so this may be why the birthplace was considered a permanent factor. In our modern, rapidly changing world, this is no longer true or necessary. As we become more and more mobile, our charts should reflect this fact.

The 4th House of Endings and Early Childhood Conditioning

Of all the angles of the birth chart, the 4th house is the most neglected and forgotten, and probably the most misunderstood of the four angular houses. Is this because it is also the house of endings, including death, the end of life? Human beings, astrologers included, tend to ignore death and the inevitable; modern society tends to encourage this attitude.

Through the efforts of a few brave pioneers such as Swiss psychiatrist Elizabeth Kubler-Ross, who interviewed dying people and investigated the cultural taboos surrounding death in her book *On Death and Dying* (and has a typical Sun/Pluto conjunction, squared by Mars), and Robert Veatch, author of *Death, Dying, and the Biological Revolution*, the word death is respectable, or at least mentionable, again. Nevertheless, the word continues to evoke fear. Ethically, modern astrologers frown upon predictions of death, so some tend to conveniently ignore the 4th house. It seems safer that way, but this doesn't lessen its significance.

Nicholas DeVore in his *Encyclopedia of Astrology* calls the 4th cusp "the degree of Integration," stating that "although it is the weakest of the four Angles, it nevertheless exercises a decisive influence throughout the entire Figure." I tend to agree with the last part of this statement while disagreeing with the first part. I believe it's time for the neglected and forgotten 4th house to take its proper place among the important angular houses and come out of the closet once and for all!

With this in mind, let's examine the meaning of the 4th house more closely. What does it rule other than death? In a natal chart, it's associated with land, property, and our home or residence—the place where one lives—as well as one's childhood birthplace or early environment. It rules the child's early life or upbringing, and the character or the environment of the home, one's roots or heritage. Since psychologists often tell us that a child's character is formed within the first four or five years or less, this house may be connected to the emotional foundation, or "emotional intelligence", of the personality. From this vantage point, the 4th house might just as well have been called the house of *beginnings* rather than the house of endings. Its importance cannot be overstated.

The Polarity between the 4th and 10th Houses

In natal astrology, the *parental angles* have always been associated with the 4th and 10th houses, and unless we arbitrarily assign more importance to one parent than the other, these houses should, in my opinion, be considered of equal importance. The 4th house cusp of the birth chart is at the Northern end of the meridian passing through the birthplace. It is sometimes called the IC or *Immum Coeli*, which is Latin for *bottom of the sky*, since it opposes the MC or *Medium Coeli*, commonly called the Midheaven, or noon point. The polarity between the 4th and 10th houses is reciprocal. The 10th is often regarded as the most powerful, but this may be because the 10th house, being above the horizon, is in the public or social arena whereas the 4th house, being below the horizon, is more private or personal. This difference, however, doesn't diminish the importance of the 4th house.

Most modern astrologers (including myself) usually assign the 10th house to the mother in a female nativity while the 4th house is assigned to the father. The rule is reversed for male birth charts; see table 2. Some other astrologers determine the selection of parental rulership based on which parent has the most authority over the child. They assign the 10th house to whichever parent is deemed to be the more significant or has the strongest influence.

As described in *Astrology;—30 Years Research*, edited and compiled by Doris C. Doane, the Church of Light in California conducted a study of the death of parents, using one hundred charts, and concluded that the 10th house always rules the mother and the 4th the father.

The only fact that the majority of astrologers generally seem to agree upon is that the 4th and 10th definitely rule the parents. As Robert Hand has pointed out in his book, *Essays on Astrology*, no absolute rules or standards have been established as yet, and this is still a controversial issue that needs further research. I prefer the modern method outlined above, which gives equal importance to both the 4th and 10th house angles, but bases rulership upon gender. This is the method I use throughout this book.

In analyzing murderers' birth charts, we find that many of them were physically or sexually abused as children, or they came from dysfunctional homes where the parents were separated or divorced. Diane Downs' chart, analyzed in Chapter 1, illustrates this type of sexual abuse, which began when she was twelve years old. The 4th house ruler, Mercury, representing her father, is conjunct a violent planet, Mars; when the alleged abuse began, her progressed Sun (male parent) had reached an exact conjunction with her natal Pluto, which suggests the possibility of rape or incest in a female birth chart.

In Chapter 3, the birth chart of another murderer, Richard Speck, shows natal Neptune exactly conjunct his Ascendant, squaring the 4th and 10th parental cusps, indicating his lifelong abuse of alcohol and drugs. His 4th house ruler, Jupiter, located in the 9th house, closely squares his Moon's Nodes and opposes his Sagittarian Sun, showing his long-lasting entanglement with the law. An affable drifter who forged checks and burglarized, Speck was already wanted for a knife assault on a woman in another state when arrested in 1966 for the mass murder of eight student nurses in Chicago. Dr. Marvin Ziporyn, a well-known psychiatrist who examined Speck in prison, reported Speck had suffered at least eight major brain concussions before age fourteen, suggesting extreme parental neglect, or physical abuse, at its worst. As an adolescent, Speck had been institutionalized in a juvenile home.

Most analysts and experts on criminal behavior agree that symptoms of disturbing behavior usually begin in childhood and often manifest as bedwetting, firesetting, and cruelty to animals. Parental neglect, sexual abuse, or brutality may cause these reactions in children and should be regarded as a danger signal. In Chapter 2, I explore the possibility that early childhood fears and traumas were a factor in the Jeffrey MacDonald murder case. MacDonald was convicted of brutally murdering his two-year-old daughter, who was having trouble with bedwetting.

The sign on the 4th house cusp is significant, as is its ruler or co-rulers, but planets within the 4th house tend to activate and modify it. By emphasizing the meaning of the 4th house, I don't mean to minimize the significance of the 10th house, since as explained above, both houses rule the parental angles, which are very important, especially to early childhood conditioning. Planets within the 10th house may also directly oppose or aspect planets in the 4th, thereby affecting them by polarity, and vice versa. The 4th rules changes in our environment and is usually aspected whenever we change locations. However, these changes don't come under our complete control until we become adults (unless we're among the few who rebel and run away from home as youngsters). Until then, because of our sustenance needs as infants or children, we're under the control of the established power structure represented by the 10th house (those in authority over us). Since human beings take such a long time to mature, this is probably for the greater good of society.

When we reach adulthood, we gradually learn to cope with, or control, our environment to some extent as our freedom increases and our need for sustenance or security decreases. For these reasons and others, the 4th house represents the early childhood home or environment, which we're powerless to change until we reach adulthood or leave home permanently. Until then, we're obliged to live in the environment provided by our parents. If we're lucky, it will be a stable environment; if not, we may be forced to adjust or suffer the consequences.

During childhood and puberty we make "inner" rather than "outer" adjustments to our environment, which may or may not be obvious or visible to others—hence, the private and personal 4th house doesn't finally come under our obvious control until we reach adulthood. As we gradually develop our social and survival skills, these inner changes can then be projected upon the outer environment and may result in our leaving the parental home or birthplace either temporarily or permanently. The 4th house ruler and/or occupants are almost always activated or heavily aspected during these times of relocation.

After all, becoming an adult usually requires that we leave our parents' home and the psychological and physical comfort and control that it represents. If for some reason we fail to make this adjustment, we may remain psychologically tied to the parental umbilical cord. Therefore, the true meaning of the 4th and 10th house polarity becomes clearer as we realize it represents a struggle to attain power, and it maps the success or failure of our attempts to do so.

Maturity, however, means responsible use of power, not its misuse. As we mature and acquire power we also take on increased social responsibilities and, hopefully, self-discipline—qualities most often associated with native 10th house ruler Capricorn and its ruling planet Saturn.

Because Saturn rules fathers and the Moon rules mothers, when an aspect such as Moon square Saturn is found in a natal chart, it suggests that physical or emotional sustenance needs were not fully met in childhood, resulting in an unnatural and prolonged state of dependency on one or both of the parents. In later years, this person often transfers their dependency to the marriage partner. Many a marriage has floundered or failed due to a spouse's refusal, or inability, to cut the umbilical cord. This isn't always the fault of the individual, since some parents unfortunately become obsessively possessive of their offspring and refuse to let them go.

Looking at this from still another viewpoint, the first quadrant, or first three houses, symbolically represents early childhood or the first seven years of life; the second quadrant represents the next seven years, ending with the fourteenth year (puberty) at the cusp of the 7th house. The 8th, 9th, and 10th houses represent ages fourteen to twenty-one, the latter being the age when our western society recognizes the person as a fully mature adult responsible for his or her own actions and choices. Depending on where our natal Moon is at birth, the progressed Moon takes approximately twenty-one years to traverse nine houses or signs of the zodiac. For example, if the Moon occupies the 10th house at birth, it will reach the 7th house of marriage in approximately twenty-one years. Not everyone, of course, is born with natal Moon in the 10th, but the cycle of approximately twenty-one years remains the same regardless.

The sign on the Midheaven, or 10th house cusp, as well as the condition of the ruling planet of that sign and its aspects, traditionally denotes the career or profession, and influences all public events connected with promotions, honor, or reputation. Often we will see the MC heavily aspected by transits or progressions when a person marries and begins to prepare for raising a family. Major transits or progressions to the 10th house also reflect a change in social status and public image. The effects of these transits on the 4th house often result in a change of residence as well, as one or both partners in a marriage relocates.

In natal chart interpretation, the 4th house represents family values, early childhood memories or conditioning, and the subconscious, private self as opposed to the public self. However, a planet within the 4th may have a profound effect on one's psyche and may find expression in one's work (10th house) or choice of career. These two houses complement each other. Their polarity, opposition, and proximity are symbolic. What's reflected or mirrored in one house may very well be expressed or projected through the opposite house.

In the past, the 4th house was associated with the mother who stayed at home and played a private role, and the 10th with the father who went to work and played a public (and dominant) one. Now, parental role reversals are becoming more commonplace. For example, after many years of being a major public figure, John Lennon, the late rock star, chose to remain at home and raise his young son while his Aquarian wife, Yoko Ono, took a more active part in public life and in handling their business affairs. Lennon's natal Moon in Aquarius trines the trailblazing and innovative planet Uranus, and rules his 4th house of domestic affairs. (Lennon was assassinated directly in front of the Dakota, the New York apartment building where he lived; see Chapter 4.)

During the advent of the industrial age, which we're slowly leaving behind us, a strong, distinct division between home and workplace may have been an absolute necessity; but now we're in transition and rapidly entering a new Age of Information (or Age of Aquarius, if you will). In the age of Uranian electronics, computers can be found in almost every home and communication is almost instantaneous, even for the physically challenged. The former isolation of and strict division between home and job, or marketplace and consumer, is disappearing on a daily basis.

Shouldn't astrology reflect this new perspective? Or will we be satisfied to dogmatize and preserve the archaic, obsolete patterns of the past?

While Uranus, astrology's ruler, occupied Capricorn, a conservative, Saturn-ruled sign, we tended to resist change. As it transits Aquarius, its "home" sign, from now until 2003, we are likely to experience a renaissance and renewal of astrology. A lot of what we now take for granted will probably be challenged, and is likely to be judged as outdated! It seems like we all need endings, and new beginnings.

Part 1:

Homicide

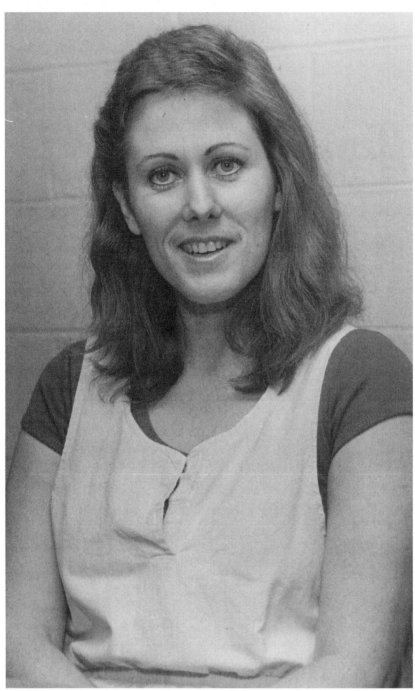

AP/ Wide World Photos

Chapter One

The Diane Downs Murder Case

A Woman Who Shot Her Children

Is the female of the species more deadly than the male? During the first half of 1989, there was a thirteen-percent increase in the female prison population. According to current statistics, however, women commit only fifteen percent of all murders.

Unlike men, when women kill, they're more likely to kill those who are closest to them, their intimates, such as husbands, lovers, and, yes, even their children. So perhaps in a sense, this does make them more deadly than the male.

In more than half of the domestic cases studied, women who killed were responding to prolonged physical abuse and were acting in self-defense. What about women who kill without any apparent motivation? And what about women who kill their own defenseless children? What category do they fall into?

Can we understand (even though we can't possibly condone) the motivation of a female who turns, or transforms, from Eve, the giver of life, into Lilith, the taker? Can a twisted, deluded woman feel that because she gave her children life, she is also justified in taking their lives?

Diane Downs made front page headlines when she was accused and convicted of shooting her three children on a lonely country road just outside Springfield, Oregon, on May 19, 1983. Seven-year-old Cheryl Downs died; the other two children were left in serious condition, with three-year-old Danny partially paralyzed. The twenty-seven-year-old mother drove the children to a hospital, where she was treated for a minor wound in her lower left arm. She claimed that a "shaggy-haired stranger" had stopped her on the road and was responsible for the crime. No such person was ever found. The investigation continued, and she was arrested and charged with the shootings nine months later, on February 28, 1984. District Attorney Fred Hugi (who later adopted her two surviving children) and the jury didn't buy her story; she was convicted of the crimes after her oldest daughter Christie testified against her at the trial. Her ex-husband and her former lover also testified.

According to Ann Rule's book *Small Sacrifices: A True Story of Passion and Murder*, Diane Elizabeth Frederickson was the oldest of five children born to Wes and Willadene Frederickson, a Southern Baptist couple. Diane was born August 7, 1955, at 7:35 P.M. MST in Phoenix, Arizona. Her birth chart (see Chart 1) shows the 20th degree of the impersonal sign, Aquarius, rising on the Ascendant, Sun in 14° Leo, and the Moon in 6° Aries. Her final dispositor is the Sun, and she has a stellium of six planets in Leo, the sign of children; Saturn, that hard taskmaster, squares all but

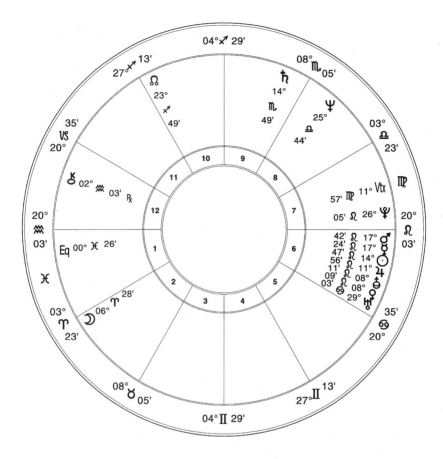

Chart 1. Natal chart for Diane Downs. Born August 7, 1955, 7:35 P.M. MST, Phoenix, AZ, 112W04, 33N27. Placidus houses. Sources: Ann Rule's book Small Sacrifices, *page 91, and "B" data from Dana Holliday in Lois Rodden's* Astro Data V; *both sources concur.*

one of her Leo planets. The ruler of her chart, Uranus, is in the critical 29th degree of Cancer, and was in exact square to transiting Saturn and Pluto on the night the crime was committed.

It is believed the crime was committed between 9:45 and 10:30 P.M. PDT on May 19, 1983, on a road outside the Springfield city limits in Marcola, Oregon. Chart 2 shows the transits for 9:55 P.M. PDT, when it is estimated that the crime occurred. Diane Downs arrived with her children at the emergency room of the McKenzie-Willamette Hospital in Oregon around 10:39 P.M. PDT, or approximately forty-four minutes

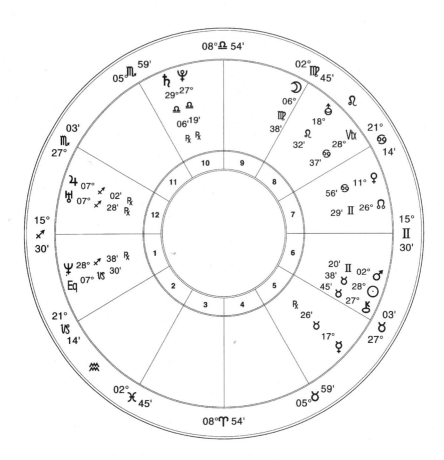

Chart 2. Event chart for the shooting. May 19, 1983, 9:55 P.M. PDT (estimated time), Marcola, OR, 122W52, 44N10. Placidus houses. Source: Ann Rules' Small Sacrifices, page 27.

after the shootings. (See Chart 3 for the transits upon her arrival.)

In 1983, Diane Downs was a divorced twenty-seven-year-old, working as a postal carrier. She liked her job because it allowed her to socialize and gave her an opportunity to meet men. Her married lover had recently moved away from Springfield, Oregon, returning to his wife and beginning a new life in another state. He wasn't particularly fond of children, and it is believed that Diane's main motive for the crime was to rid herself of her children so she'd appear more attractive to him. She feared the separation was permanent, but was trying desperately to effect a reconciliation. His

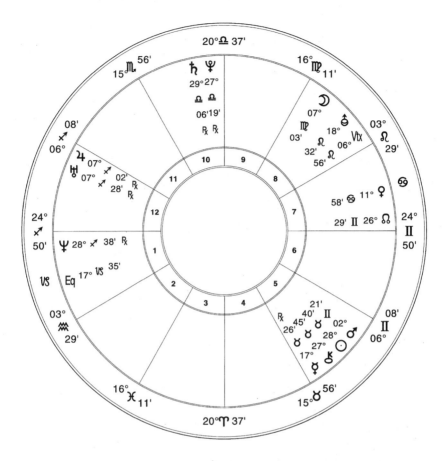

Chart 3. *Event chart for Diane's arrival at hospital. May 19, 1983, 10:39 P.M. PDT, Spring-field, OR, 123W01, 44N03. Placidus houses. Source: Ann Rule's* Small Sacrifices, *page 12.*

mind was made up, though, and so far, nothing she'd done had seemed to please him.

Diane was not one to give up easily, however, with her natal Moon in 6° Aries and the Moon's dispositor, Mars, closely conjunct her Leo Sun. She has an assertive, extroverted type of personality and enjoys being the center of attention. Natal Sun opposite her Ascendant bestows a strong ego with the need to be considered important. Her Ascendant ruler, Uranus, occupies the critical 29th degree of Cancer, and squares Neptune in her 8th house. Neptune rules the intercepted sign of Pisces in her large

1st house. She had indulged in several love affairs in the two years prior to separating from her ex-husband, Steven Downs, in 1981. She was not one to deprive herself of male companionship or sex.

According to her own statements, Diane was prematurely introduced to sex as a twelve-year-old, when her father began to abuse her sexually. The progressed Sun (denoting the father) had moved to 26° Leo that year, making an exact conjunction with natal Pluto in her 7th house, which testifies to the truth of her statements. Her Mars/Uranus midpoint at 8° Leo exactly conjoins her natal Venus and Transpluto, indicating the strong possibility of being a rape victim during her lifetime. Mercury rules the 4th house (the male parent) and is afflicted by an exact conjunction to Mars and a square to Saturn. Her natal Sun, also representing the males in her life, is closely conjunct Mars and square Saturn, showing cruelty. At age thirteen, when the progressed MC was trine her Mercury-Mars conjunction, she cut her wrists in an attempt to commit suicide.

While in high school, at age fifteen, Diane met her husband-to-be, Steve Downs. On November 13, 1973, when both were only eighteen, she left home to marry Steve, who was working as a model. He was born January 12, 1955 (time unknown), in Chandler, Arizona.

Diane has no Earth planets in her chart; Steve has both Sun and Moon in Earth signs, having Sun in Capricorn and Moon in Virgo, offering down-to-earth stability. Although they have many similar slow-moving planetary placements because of their age similarity, Steve's chart contains only one Leo planet, Pluto. There's little compatibility between their charts except for his Jupiter conjunct her natal Uranus. His Sun in Capricorn opposes her Uranus, a separative, although exciting, aspect, so their marriage lasted only about eight years.

Although we don't know the exact time of Steve's birth, we know his natal Moon is definitely in Virgo, and when comparing his chart to Diane's, we see that his Moon falls in her natal 7th house of partnerships. When they were married in 1973, her progressed Sun was just entering Virgo, indicating a short-lived, temporary compatibility based on her progressed aspects. Diane's progressed Midheaven was conjunct her North Node (relationships), and natal Mercury and Mars were both inconjunct her progressed Ascendant. Mercury rules the intercepted sign of Virgo on her 7th house of marriage, and also rules her 5th house of progeny.

The couple lived in Arizona until they separated and divorced around 1981. Diane moved to Oregon in March 1983.

The union produced three children (though apparently not all the children had the same father). The first two children were born in Chandler, Arizona, as follows: Christie Ann Downs, born October 7, 1974, and Cheryl Downs, born January 10, 1976. The youngest child, Stephen Daniel, was born on December 29, 1979, in Tempe, Arizona. Diane is also known to have had a child as a surrogate mother.

In 1988, when she appeared on the Oprah Winfrey show from her prison cell, Diane claimed she'd been pregnant five times altogether. At the time of her trial, she was eight or nine months pregnant. Shortly thereafter, she gave birth to an illegitimate female child on June 27, 1984, in Eugene, Oregon. This child was put up for adoption. According to data given in Ann Rule's book *Small Sacrifices*, Diane's daughter, named Amy Elizabeth, was born at 10:06 P.M. PDT. See Chart 4, where I have rectified her birth chart by the prenatal epoch. Amy has Sun in Cancer and Moon in Gemini. This Sun/Moon configuration is known as the dark of the Moon—or the period just before a New Moon. Amy has a Capricorn Ascendant. The child was evidently deliberately conceived on October 13, 1983, just four months before Diane's arrest, when she abruptly visited Matt Jensen's apartment around midnight because she thought she was in her fertile period. Obsessed with becoming pregnant again, she felt it was her only salvation. Diane has been quoted as saying she never "felt better than when she was pregnant."

For those of you who use the *prenatal epoch* method (see glossary), developed by E. H. Bailey, these two charts fully confirm his method. Is this only a coincidence? Decide for yourself, but the dates are nevertheless similar, as you can see from the following data. According to Bailey's rules, as presented in *The Prenatal Epoch*, Amy's epoch (see Chart 5), signifying ovulation or conception, falls on exactly the same date, October 13, 1983, at 9:43:05 P.M. PD. This is the time when Diane claims to have visited Jensen's apartment. In fact, the calculated epoch is just one hour and seventeen minutes before the time Diane claims to have visited Jensen and had intercourse with him. In Ann Rule's book *Small Sacrifices*, the author

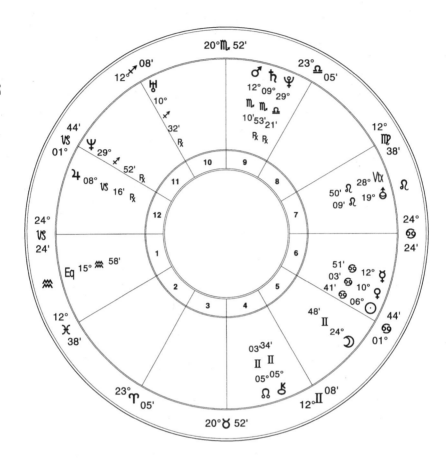

Chart 4. Rectified natal chart for Amy Elizabeth Downs. Born June 27, 1984, 10:00:04 P.M. PDT, Eugene, OR, 123W04, 44N05. Source: Ann Rule's Small Sacrifices, page 460. Rectified by prenatal epoch, six minutes less than given time (10:06 P.M.) on page 460 of Rule's book.

states, "It was after 11:00 P.M. PDT when Diane visited her lover."

Amy's *rectified* Ascendant is 24°24' Capricorn, or six minutes earlier than the time given for her birth in Ann Rule's book. (Rule gives 10:06 P.M.). If the corresponding female epoch with the Moon in 24°24' Capricorn and Ascendant at 24°48' Gemini is accepted as correct, the *rectified* time of birth is 10:00 P.M. PDT, as shown by Chart 4.

Amy's epoch should be erected for Cottage Grove, Oregon: Longitude 123W03/Latitude 43N48. The rules for a 4th Order type of birth—

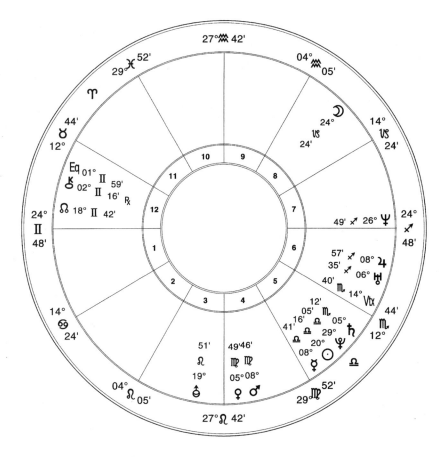

*Chart 5. Prenatal epoch for Amy Elizabeth. October 13, 1983, 9:43:05 P.M. PDT,
Cottage Grove, OR, 123W03, 43N48. Placidus houses. Source: Ann Rules' Small Sacrifices,
pages 281-282. Book gives the date of intercourse with her lover, and probable conception date.*

when the natal Moon is below the horizon and decreasing—indicate a
gestation period of fewer than 273 days. *The Prenatal Epoch* provides instructions for rectifying birth times and states Bailey's belief that the
epoch probably represents ovulation rather than the moment of conception. This particular case history would certainly seem to demonstrate or
confirm Bailey's theory, since the timing of the epoch is about one hour
before intercourse occurred. Both events occurred on exactly the same
date, so I believe this makes them doubly significant.

Some astrologers are inclined to discard the prenatal epoch technique, claiming that it's an outdated method that seldom works. I can't help but wonder whether they have ever actually tried the method! After overcoming some of the initial difficulties of learning to use this technique properly, I must admit I've had good results when the birth time is known within an hour.

According to Reinhold Ebertin in *The Combination of Stellar Influences*, the Mars/Jupiter midpoint represents "the ability to procreate or beget children." In Diane's birth chart, this fertility midpoint at 14°49' Leo is highly activated; the midpoint is exactly conjunct her Sun at 14°48' Leo, within a three-degree orb of her 5th house ruler, Mercury, representing children in her chart. Amy's natal Equatorial Ascendant (EP), at 15°58' Aquarius, is just one degree from an opposition aspect to this "fertility" point in her mother's chart. The mother's Sun/Moon midpoint at 10° Gemini is exactly opposed by the daughter's natal Uranus, signifying an instant separation at birth. Amy was given up for adoption immediately after being born to her imprisoned mother.

Diane Downs' successful rate of childbearing made her a prime candidate for surrogate motherhood. Just before midnight on May 7, 1982, in Louisville, Kentucky, Diane gave birth to a baby girl. The child was given up for adoption to surrogate parents who paid Diane ten thousand dollars for her labor and sacrifice. Part of this money was spent on a trailer, since she had permanently separated from her husband and needed a place to live. Shortly after, Diane and her sister attempted to organize a surrogate clinic of their own, but this idea was reluctantly abandoned when they were unable to comply with restrictive state regulations.

Diane's natal 5th house ruler, Mercury, is conjunct the violent planet Mars (her Moon's dispositor), and her Venus is conjunct Transpluto, so her children were exposed to her violent impulses and were her prime targets. The hypothetical planet Transpluto is the higher octave of Jupiter and denotes sudden releases of energy.

According to the precepts of Uranian astrology, the Mars/Pluto midpoint signifies murder, violent assaults, and brutality. Diane's natal Mars/Pluto midpoint at 21°53' Leo directly opposes her Ascendant at 20°03' Aquarius. Diane's natal Mercury/Mars conjunction at 17° Leo, in

Chart 6. Diane's chart progressed to the date of daughter Cheryl's death. Progressions for May 19, 1983, 9:55 P.M. PDT (estimated time), Marcola, OR 122W52, 44N10. Placidus houses.

opposition to her Ascendant and square Saturn, makes her a compulsive talker. She is a moody, self-centered individual, and a liar who tends to rationalize everything she does. The numerous Saturn squares to her stellium of natal planets in Leo (including Venus, Jupiter, Sun, Mercury, and Mars), make her subject to periodic fits of deep depression followed by elation. Jupiter/Saturn afflictions, especially squares and oppositions, often indicate a see-saw, manic-depressive type of personality.

At the same time, she is said to have an IQ of 125 on the Wechsler Intelligence Scale. Although she may be above average in intelligence, emotionally she still seems to be a child—probably an abused child who was forced to mature too quickly and was introduced to sex prematurely. Transpluto at 8° Leo, exactly conjunct her natal Venus, and Venus conjunct Mars, makes her prone to sudden fits of violence and anger, although she can project a sexy, charismatic personality when it suits her purposes. In 1983, on the day she and her three children were shot, Transpluto was at 18° Leo, sitting on her natal Mercury/Mars conjunction and opposite her Ascendant at 20° Aquarius. Transiting Mercury at 17° Taurus squared Transpluto and her Mercury/Mars conjunction. Transpluto conjunct Mars is a potentially dangerous aspect; it is one of the worst for violent crimes such as murder.

On May 19, 1983, the day her daughter Cheryl died of two gunshot wounds, Diane's progressed Moon at 13° Aries trined her natal Sun in Leo, but the Moon was also inconjunct natal Saturn and progressed Venus, and sesquiquadrate her natal Pluto; see Chart 6. Progressed Mercury at 4° Libra, ruler of both her 4th (death) and 5th (children) houses, conjoins her natal 8th house cusp. When she was arrested on February 28, 1984, her progressed Ascendant opposed this point at 3° Aries, and the progressed Moon at 24° Aries was applying to an opposition to her natal Neptune in the 8th.

Progressed Sun at 11° Virgo and Venus at 12° Virgo conjoin her natal Vertex in the 7th house; these two planets are semisquare natal Neptune and square the transiting Ascendant at the time of the crime. One of the most difficult aspects in her chart is the square of Uranus and Neptune, since these planets are the co-rulers of her ascending signs, Aquarius and Pisces. On the day of the crime, her progressed Sun and Venus were conjunct her Uranus/Neptune midpoint at 12° Virgo.

Chart 2 shows the transits for the date of the crime even more precisely, with the Moon at 6° Virgo conjunct her progressed Mars at 5° Virgo, square transiting Uranus and Jupiter near her natal Midheaven. Mars/Uranus aspects often precede accidents or sudden violent incidents. Transiting Saturn at 29° Libra, co-ruler of Diane's Aquarius Ascendant, exactly squares her other impulsive Ascendant ruler, Uranus, and is conjunct natal Neptune—the planet ruling illusions and delusions—in her 8th house. Transiting Neptune in 28° Sagittarius is exactly opposite her prenatal eclipse point of 28°05' Gemini on the cusp of her 5th house, and inconjunct her natal Uranus. These aspects are tight and very precise.

During this stressful period, her natal Uranus/Neptune square was being activated by transits from two slow-moving planets, Saturn and Pluto, so these aspects were long-lasting rather than temporary. Transiting Pluto, the planet of death and transition at 27° Libra squares her natal Uranus, sextiles her natal Pluto, and conjoins natal Neptune at 25° Libra in her 8th house of death and sex. The transiting Saturn aspects accent her depressed mental condition and inability to face reality. Saturn conjunct Neptune, or afflicting Neptune, is seldom a pleasant experience since it requires a strict allegiance to the hard facts of life as demonstrated by Saturn, rather than indulgence in Neptune's world of make-believe. This aspect can be used positively if the individual avoids wishful thinking or indulging in fantasy, and adheres to a realistic analysis of facts; unfortunately, that's seldom the case.

At the estimated time of the shootings, about 9:55 P.M. PDT on May 19, 1983, 15° Sagittarius is on the Ascendant and the 1st house holds transiting Neptune conjunct the South Node within 25–28° Sagittarius. Transiting Neptune and the Nodes are inconjunct Diane's natal Uranus, conjunct her natal 11th house of hopes and wishes, and opposite the cusp of her 5th house of children. Those Saturn/Neptune aspects (fantasy versus reality) are again accented in the transiting chart, as the transiting Saturn/Neptune midpoint at 28° Scorpio is exactly opposite transiting Sun at 28° Taurus and the planet Lilith at 28° Taurus. Lilith, according to author/astrologer Ivy Jacobson, is the taker of life, in contrast to the Sun, which is the giver. Diane's natal Lilith is located at 20° Aries, opposite natal Neptune in the 8th house

Epilogue

After her trial in May 1984, and conviction of murder on June 17, 1984, at 12:20 A.M. in Springfield, Oregon, Diane was confined to the Oregon Correctional Institute for Women to serve a life sentence, plus sixty-five years. However, on July 11, 1987, around 8:40 A.M. PDT, she escaped from prison. After an extensive search, police found her ten days later in a locked bedroom with one of four men who lived in the house. The man turned out to be the estranged husband of one of her cell mates. Evidently, she was up to her old tricks, trying desperately to get pregnant again.

When questioned, Diane claimed she was trying to get to California to look for "the man who killed her children." She still sticks to her story about the bearded stranger who assaulted her children, and she shows no remorse for the crimes for which she has been convicted.

While in prison, Diane has been diagnosed as suffering from a personality disorder and having a narcissistic type of personality. She keeps a diary, and when she appeared on the Oprah Winfrey show in 1988 with Ann Rule, author of *Small Sacrifices*, she stated rather defensively that Ann Rule had never even interviewed her for that book. She said another book, entitled *Best Kept Secrets*, would be published in November–December of 1989 and would reveal her secrets, giving her side of the story. [This book does not appear in *Books in Print*. Ed.]

After her escape from the Oregon prison, she was moved to the Clinton Correctional Institute for Women in New Jersey, where she now resides. With Chiron at 2° Aquarius occupying her 12th house at birth, prison could be therapeutic for her, but she'd probably mourn the loss of her freedom, since Chiron, planet of healing, makes an out-of-sign opposition to her Ascendant ruler, Uranus, within her 6th house.

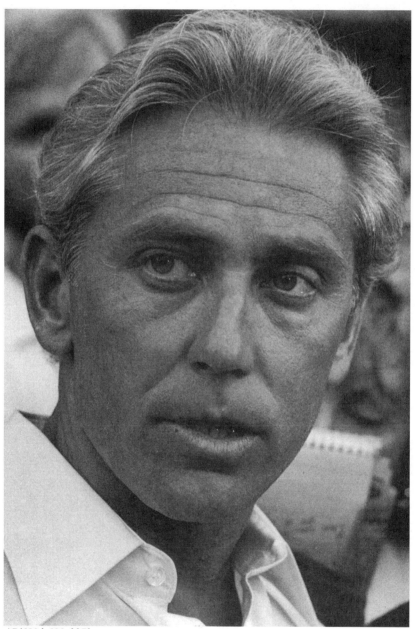

AP/ Wide World Photos

Chapter Two

Who Was the "Fatal Vision" Murderer?

New Insights into the Jeffrey MacDonald Murder Case

The "Fatal Vision" murder case may be over as far as the trial and conviction of former Green Beret Dr. Jeffrey MacDonald is concerned, but the mystery remains. MacDonald still insists that he is innocent, and there are many unanswered questions about the crime. MacDonald is serving three consecutive life terms for his conviction in 1979; he was accused and convicted of the slayings of his pregnant wife, Colette, and two young daughters in Fort Bragg, North Carolina, on the night of February 16, 1970.

Nine months after the murders, while still in the military, MacDonald was acquitted of the charges. After his discharge from the Army, he moved to California on July 5, 1971, where he served as director of emergency medicine at St. Mary's Hospital in Long Beach, California. He was an instructor at the UCLA medical school and a nationally known lecturer on the recognition and treatment of child abuse. When not working, he led the good life of the perennial bachelor, spending most of his weekends on his motorboat with his latest girlfriend.

Nine years later, on August 19, 1979, his luck ran out. He was brought to trial again, this time as a civilian. The arrest was due to a determined investigation by his father-in-law, a former supporter. Alfred Kassab had begun to suspect that MacDonald was not just one of the victims of a horrible crime but was perhaps the *perpetrator* of the crimes. Once convinced, he was willing to take the case to the Supreme Court, if necessary, to see that justice was done.

Colette was Mildred Kassab's only child by a previous marriage; her stepfather adored her. Her youthful death at the age of twenty-six was a tragic blow to the Kassabs, and they couldn't stop grieving the loss of their only daughter and their precious grandchildren.

The couple had been high school sweethearts and had previously obtained the support of both families for their marriage, although they had planned to wait until MacDonald completed his medical education at Princeton University. Collette was already pregnant with their first child, Kimberly, when Kassab led his stepdaughter down the aisle in a hasty Greenwich Village church ceremony in September 1963.

Jeff was an ambitious, handsome young man who was planning to become a physician. The families realized there would be hard times ahead financially for the young couple, but Jeff and Colette appeared to be deeply in love with each other. The option of abortion had apparently not entered their minds, perhaps because MacDonald was a Catholic.

According to Rodden's *Astro Data III*, Jeffrey MacDonald was born on

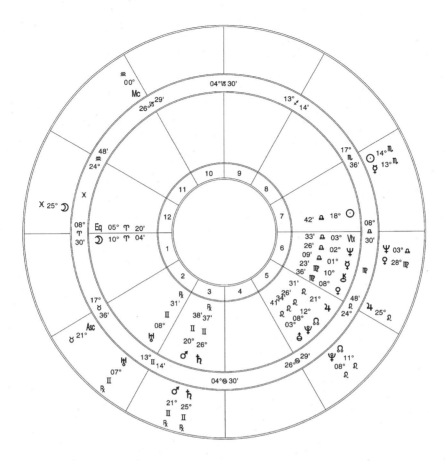

Chart 7. Natal chart for Jeffrey MacDonald, progressed to February 16, 1970, the date of the murders. Born on October 12, 1943, 5:53 P.M. EWT, New York, NY, 73W57, 40N45. Placidus houses. Source: Data from birth certificate, Lois Rodden's Astro Data III, page 129.

October 12, 1943, at 5:53 P.M. EWT, in New York, New York. This "A" data is from the birth certificate. Chart 7 shows his Sun in 18° Libra opposing his Moon and Ascendant in the fiery Mars-ruled Aries rising sign. He is a Full Moon type. His ruler, Mars, is conjunct Saturn in Gemini in the 3rd house and trines his Sun. He wanted to be a surgeon (Mars rules cutting instruments). Mars and Saturn aspects are often prominent in the charts of those who practice medicine.

Since Colette's hour of birth is not known to us at this time, we will use a sunrise chart (4:45:34 A.M. EST) for her date of birth on May 10,

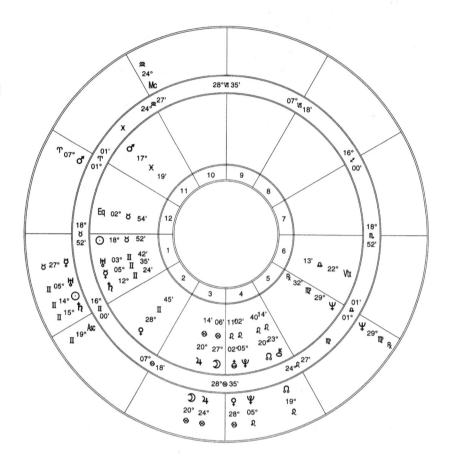

Chart 8. Sunrise chart for Colette MacDonald, progressed to the date of the murder, February 16, 1970. Born May 10, 1943; time unknown. Chart calculated for 4:45:34 A.M. EST, Patchogue, NY, 73W01, 40N46. Source: Reported birth date from Joe McGinniss, Fatal Vision, page 82.

1943, in Patchogue, New York; see Chart 8. Her birth date is given in Joe McGinniss' book *Fatal Vision*. Colette's 7th house ruler, Mars, is sextile her natal Sun in 18° Taurus, indicating her initial interest in becoming a doctor's wife; but her Moon's Nodes square her Sun (5th house ruler), so her children gradually became her main interest in life.

Kimberly's birth on April 18, 1964, was followed by the birth of another girl, named Kristen, in May of 1967. Both children were born by Caesarean section and Colette experienced various difficulties in childbirth. When she married Jeff at age twenty in 1963, her solar arc-progressed

Midheaven squared her natal Sun. A year or so later, it moved within orb of a conjunction to her 5th house Nodes in Aquarius and Leo, a T-square in fixed signs.

Colette was an intelligent woman who was a stay-at-home mother (Moon in Cancer) throughout most of her marriage. As she matured, she was anxious to add to her knowledge through self-study and continuing education. Her Mercury conjunct Uranus testifies to this strong sense of curiosity. Uranus and Saturn contain her Mercury in Gemini, so she had a stable but penetrating mentality.

Early on the night of the murders, Colette was attending a class in child psychology. She returned home about 9:40 P.M. EST on February 16, 1970, after driving a friend home from class. She confided in her friend before they parted that she was concerned about her husband's exhausted condition; that he had worked all night the night before and then worked almost all the next day. It seems, however, that this was nothing unusual, as he had a rigorous schedule and did a lot of moonlighting. She also said she was worried because her husband had told her he might be joining a boxing team that was going to Russia.

She was pregnant with their third child, expecting the baby in July, and was afraid her husband might not return in time for the baby's birth. It was important to her that he be there, as he had been for the birth of their other two children. Her mother, who lived in another state, had promised to be there in Jeff's stead, but this arrangement was not entirely acceptable to Colette. It's probable that they discussed the matter again on the night of her death, although Jeff claims his memory is vague on this point.

MacDonald claims he and Colette talked for a while, and that she retired for bed early. He stayed up to watch a late television show. Later, when he entered the master bedroom, he found his two-year-old child, Kristen, sleeping in bed with her mother. Kristen had urinated on his place in the bed, so he decided to sleep on the couch rather than disturb his wife by changing the sheets. MacDonald said the bed-wetting happened frequently and that the youngest child often slept in their bed, although both girls had their own bedrooms.

He told the police that Colette may have mentioned to her psychology instructor the problem they were having with Kristen's bed-wetting and the child's recent tendency to want to sleep in her parents' bed. He claimed this occurred about "once a week," and admitted that he and his wife had different ideas about how to solve the problem.

Colette, who was usually not active in class discussions, had indeed posed a question regarding the issue to her instructor. "She raised the question," her friend said, "about her youngest child coming into bed with her and her husband in the night. She wondered whether they should allow the little girl to stay the night or if they should put her back in bed. It seemed her husband felt the little girl should stay in bed with him, and she (Colette) should sleep on the couch."

The very next day, Colette's friend learned that Colette and her two children, Kimberly, five years old, and Kristen, two years old, had been brutally murdered in their home on Castle Drive.

What *really* happened between 9:40 P.M. on February 16, 1970, when Colette returned home from her psychology class, and the early morning hours the next day, between 3:40 A.M. and 3:42 A.M., when the police received an emergency phone call from Jeffrey MacDonald reporting the stabbings? See Chart 9 for the transits.

When the police arrived, they found MacDonald, dressed only in his blue pajama bottoms, unconscious on the bedroom floor next to his wife. A small kitchen paring knife lay on the floor beside them. The word "Pig" was written on the headboard in blood. MacDonald was taken to a hospital immediately. A small wound in the right side of his chest was the only injury that needed immediate attention, although he was observed to be disturbed and somewhat disoriented. His wife and children were dead, battered almost beyond recognition. Three weapons were found: a blood-stained club, an ice pick, and a paring knife. At 8:00 A.M. EST, the three bodies were removed. Autopsies were later performed, and Colette's unborn child, a four-and-a-half-month-old male fetus, was removed from her womb. Funeral services were held on February 21, 1970.

MacDonald was the sole survivor of the crime, which he claimed was due to drug-crazed hippies, as in the recent Tate-LaBianca murders. Was his version of what happened that night just a clever cover-up for a brutal domestic murder? It's difficult to know the truth. There were no witnesses, although a neighbor claimed she heard the sounds of a heated dispute from the MacDonald's side of their duplex apartment wall that night. She also stated that she heard Colette threatening to kill if her children were harmed. Other neighbors claimed they heard nothing, and no one

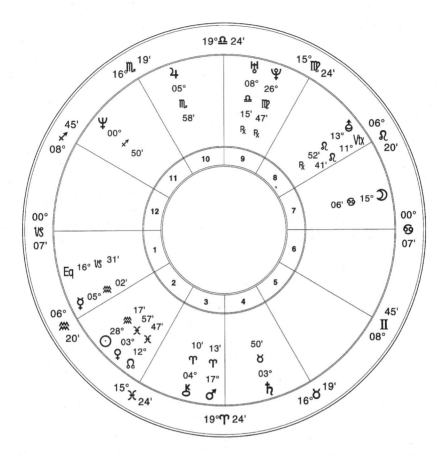

Chart 9. *Event chart for MacDonald's call to police, February 17, 1970, 3:40 A.M. EST, Fort Bragg, NC, 79W00, 35N09. Placidus houses. Source: Joe McGinniss,* Fatal Vision, *page 13.*

suspicious was observed entering or leaving the house that night.

Let's examine Chart 7 for clues to MacDonald's personality. According to the noted astrologer Charles Carter, Moon square or opposite Mercury or Neptune is often the signature of an excellent and clever liar. MacDonald's Mercury/Neptune in the 1st decanate of Libra is opposite his natal Moon in Aries. At the time of the murder, his progressed Midheaven was trine this Mercury/Neptune conjunction in his 6th house of health. Neptune also has rulership over drugs, and it was reported that MacDonald had recently lost over twenty pounds and had been going for long periods without sleep, which indicates that he may have been taking diet pills or amphetamines during this period. (In 1970, amphetamines were not necessarily considered dangerous drugs, since less was known about their potential hazards.)

On the night of the murders, MacDonald's progressed Moon at 25° Pisces was applying to a square of his natal Saturn, ruler of his 10th house of reputation, indicating a possible fall from status and the fear of a loss of professional standing. Transiting Pluto at 26° Virgo was conjunct progressed Venus, opposite his progressed Moon and square his Saturn, setting the scene for a violent confrontation as this Mutable T-Square configuration was activated by transiting Pluto on the night of February 16th.

Looking at MacDonald's progressions, we see that his progressed Moon, in his 12th house of self-undoing, squares natal Saturn. The Moon's square to Mars just five months before the crime (around the time his wife conceived) makes the release of intensely obsessive and violent impulses more likely, and also indicates the possibility of some type of addiction. Whether or not this was the potential motive for the crime is something the reader will have to decide. MacDonald's 7th house ruler, Venus, signifying his wife, has progressed to 28° Virgo where it conjoins the transiting planet of death, Pluto.

On the fatal night she was murdered, transiting Pluto at 26° Virgo was conjunct Colette's natal Neptune and sextile her natal Moon in 27° Cancer. Her Cancer Moon is near the cusp of her 4th house, the house of endings. Mars and Pluto are co-rulers of her Scorpio 7th house cusp, signifying her husband. The transiting Moon in Cancer trines her natal Mars. At age twenty-six, Colette's progressed Moon also occupied Cancer, and was just six months from making its first return to its natal position. Colette's progressed Venus at 28° Cancer is exactly conjunct her solar 4th house cusp and sextile transiting Pluto.

Further examination of Colette's progressions at the time of the murder, which probably took place around midnight of February 16-17, indicates that her progressed Mars at 7° Aries was applying to an exact conjunction with her husband's natal Aries Ascendant at 8° Aries—certainly not the best aspect for promoting marital harmony between spouses, since this involves the cusp of the 7th house also! Transiting Uranus at 8° Libra was opposite her progressed Mars and exactly conjunct her husband's

7th house cusp, indicating marital quarrels, accidents, and possible separation or divorce. Her progressed Ascendant at 19° Gemini (see Chart 8) is just past the square to her natal Mars, probably signifying bitter marital quarrels during the past two years. MacDonald's natal Mars at 20° Gemini conjunct her progressed Ascendant adds more disharmony.

At birth, Colette's 7th house ruler, Mars, was square Saturn. A violent death is a possibility, as this aspect warns against the danger of violent confrontations or arguments, especially with the spouse. This latter aspect is also known to promote repressed anger and sometimes a "revenge is sweet" attitude. It's interesting to note that MacDonald's chart contains a vindictive, vengeful Mars/Saturn aspect as well, although in a different sign, Gemini, and as a conjunction with a six-degree orb between these two natal planets.

Uranian astrologers, incidentally, claim that the negative connotations of Mars/Pluto and Saturn/Pluto midpoints can signify murder, while Mars/Uranus midpoints indicate accidents and/or injuries. Near midnight on February 16, 1970, the transiting Moon at 13° Cancer was at the midpoint of Jeffrey MacDonald's natal Mars and Pluto, and approaching a square to transiting Mars at 17° Aries. Mars was, in turn, directly opposite his natal Sun in 18° Libra, making a Cardinal T-Cross pattern in his horoscope, which calls for decisive action.

Just a few months before the murders, on November 7, 1969, MacDonald's older brother, Jay, experienced a schizophrenic break with reality and was confined to a mental hospital. Note, incidentally, that MacDonald's Mars/Saturn conjunction falls in his 3rd house of brothers and sisters. His mother, Dorothy MacDonald, a Gemini, called upon him to take care of his brother's hospitalization. MacDonald obediently went out of town to make the necessary arrangements and then became extremely depressed after he returned to his wife and children in Fort Bragg, North Carolina. Later, when Jay heard that his brother, Jeff, had been arrested and was being held by the military police, he suffered a relapse. Born only a year and a half apart, the brothers were apparently very close.

Jeffrey MacDonald was found guilty by a federal court on August 28, 1979, and is now in the Federal Corrections Institute at Bastrop, Texas, serving three life terms.

In summing up, I'd like to mention the many similarities between this case and the Sheppard murder case. Dr. Sam Sheppard was accused of murdering his wife on July 4, 1954. He was born December 29, 1923. Both Sheppard and MacDonald were doctors, highly esteemed in their community. Both wives were pregnant and clubbed to death, although in the Sheppard case the murder weapon was never recovered. Dr. Sheppard was found guilty, served ten years in prison, and was eventually acquitted after his second trial with the help of his attorney, F. Lee Bailey.

A great deal of mystery continues to surround both of these murders, which took place in supposedly safe domestic surroundings. Something we believe in as almost sacred was desecrated in both cases. Maybe this is one of the reasons the horror of these crimes lives on even after justice has been administered by the courts and the legal system.

AP/ Wide World Photos

Chapter Three

Richard Speck

Mass Murderer of Eight Nurses

Richard Speck's conspicuous tattoo "Born to Raise Hell" on his left forearm was a dead give-away, making him easy to identify and apprehend. After a three-day search for the suspected killer, the police were tipped off, and Speck was arrested at a Cook

County Hospital, where he had been taken for treatment of injuries related to a suicide attempt.

He was wanted for the gruesome massacre of eight young student nurses in their dormitory in Chicago, Illinois, around midnight of July 13–14,
1966. All eight students were either brutally strangled or stabbed to
death; only one survived.

The one who escaped death was Corazon Amurao, a young woman
from rural Batangas, a province some sixty miles from Manila. She was
one of three Philippine exchange students who had come to Chicago two
months earlier to complete nurse's training. In 1966, she was twenty-two
years old and was described as a "shy, modest, country girl." Amurao was
the first person Speck approached after illegally forcing his way into the
two-story apartment building at 2319 East 100th Street. She noticed a
strong odor of alcohol on the intruder's breath.

The killer entered the Jeffrey Manor townhouse by a back door, then
entered Miss Amurao's bedroom armed with a pistol and a knife, and
forced her to take him to the other girls' bedrooms. He gathered the girls
into one room where he gagged them and tied their palms together with
strips of sheets, using a square sailor's knot, which helped police to identify him as a seagoing type of person.

Speck then left them to wait for three other girls who were out late—
Sue Farris, Mary Jordan, and Gloria Jean Davy. The latter was reported as
Speck's first victim, and the only one who was raped. Later, it was learned
that she bore a marked resemblance to Speck's ex-wife, Shirley.

The slayings occurred early on the morning of July 14th after the three
girls returned and were bound and gagged with the others. The killer took
their money, saying he needed it to go to New Orleans to look for a job.
At first, the girls weren't aware of what was actually taking place, as Speck
systematically removed them one by one from the room and murdered
them individually. Amurao said she attempted to persuade the other girls
to gang up on the intruder and try to escape; however, the majority of the
girls were convinced that the man was only a burglar and wasn't violent.
They seemed to feel that if they remained quiet and calm, he would leave
after they gave him the money he demanded.

Having failed to convince the others, Amurao managed to roll under a

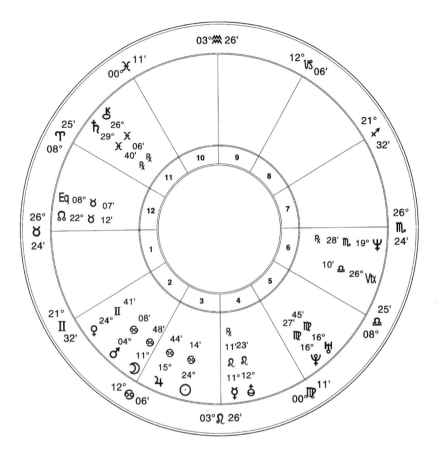

Chart 10. *Event chart for Richard Speck's arrest on July 17, 1966, 1:35 A.M. CDT, Chicago, IL 87W39, 41N52. Placidus houses. Source: Time magazine article, dated July 29, 1966.*

bed and hide. She remained frozen in this position for five or six hours, and didn't emerge from her hiding place until an alarm clock went off at about 5:00 A.M. the next morning (July 14th). It was then that she discovered the bodies of her friends and classmates. She managed to free herself, walk out on the balcony of the second-floor apartment, and scream for help, saying, "All my friends are dead! I'm the only one alive!"

Shortly after the murders, Amurao was hospitalized and treated for shock, but she was able to talk to the police and give them several helpful leads during their three-day search for the suspect. Her description of the killer proved especially helpful to the police, leading them to focus their investigations on ex-convict Speck. A sketch based on her description was immediately released to the newspapers.

A picture of Speck was published in a Chicago newspaper from a small photo he had left at a nearby Maritime Union Hall. (A few days earlier, Speck had gone to the Maritime Hall to get a job on a boat sailing down the Mississippi River to New Orleans. Probably, it was around this time that he began "stalking" the nurses' dormitory, which was directly across the street, and perhaps watching the nurses sunbathe in the back yard.)

The killer was spotted by a surgeon, Dr. LeRoy Smith, who had seen the newspaper photo of Speck. Dr. Smith identified a suicidal patient brought to the emergency room of the Cook County Hospital about 1:35 A.M. on July 17th as Richard Speck; see Chart 10. While bandaging the man's arm, the surgeon discovered a distinctive tattoo which read "Born to Raise Hell," and after asking the man if he was, indeed, Richard Speck, he told the attending nurse to call the police. Shortly thereafter, the killer was apprehended and an armed guard was placed at the hospital to prevent his escape.

According to Lois Rodden's *Astro Data II*, Speck's time of birth is recorded on his birth certificate as 1:00 A.M. CST. He was born on December 6, 1941 in Kirkwood, Illinois, a small town near Monmouth, to Mary Margaret and Benjamin Speck.

Speck's natal chart (see Chart 11) reveals the psychological make-up and inner motivations of an individual dominated mainly by the negative influence of an afflicted Neptune. Speck, however, is not a Neptune-ruled Pisces type. The opposite sign, Virgo, is rising at his birth.

His Ascendant is at 29° Virgo, a "critical" degree. Neptune conjuncts the Ascendant degree and squares all four angular house cusps. The influence of Neptune is unfortunate in his chart because this planet is in the opposite sign to which it rules, or in its detriment.

Mercury, Speck's Ascendant ruler, occupies 5° Sagittarius, conjunct the Sun at 13° Sagittarius in his 3rd house, and trine Pluto. Natal Moon at 10° Cancer is inconjunct the Sun. Neptune at 29° Virgo is closely conjunct the Equatorial Ascendant and opposes the Pisces Vertex. Since Neptune is a slow-moving outer planet, it will remain near the Ascendant throughout Speck's lifetime. Neptune's favorable trine aspects from

Chart 11. Richard Speck's natal chart. Born December 6, 1941, 1:00 A.M. CST, Kirkwood, IL, 90W45, 40N52. Placidus houses. Source: Lois Rodden's Astro Data II; from birth certificate.

Venus, Saturn, and Uranus, respectively, are canceled out by the unfavorable aspects to the four angular house cusps. Nevertheless, Neptune is powerful because it occupies the 1st house cusp.

Before analyzing this horoscope, it's important to realize that Richard Speck claims to have no memory of committing the crime he was convicted of. Is he telling the truth? [Editor's Note: The recent release of a film interview of Richard Speck conducted by a fellow prison inmate reveals that he did in fact recall and admit to the murders.]

According to Speck, his first recollection on the day after the crime was committed is waking in his boarding-house room to find a gun in one hand and blood stains on the other. He repeatedly stated that he had no idea how he obtained the gun. Speck, like many convicted criminals awaiting appeal, claimed to have no recollection of having committed a crime. He read about the murders in a newspaper the next day and only then realized he was a wanted man. Although he has apparently accepted the fact that he committed the crimes, he doesn't know why he did it and denies that the murders were premeditated. Despite this, he claims to remember some of the events leading up to the fatal killings. According to Speck, he was visiting a bar with some other sailors and was on a drinking bout. Later, he left the bar with his companions to get a "fix"; an injection of drugs.

Since drugs and narcotics come under the direct rulership of Neptune, this planet's dominant position in his chart indicates their importance in his life. Neptune rising, or dominant, usually indicates (on the negative plane) a person addicted to either drugs or alcohol as a form of escape from reality, providing Neptune is badly afflicted. Speck's record shows that he used drugs frequently and liked to drink as well. His natal Moon squares Mars, indicating the drinking habit he failed to overcome. Just preceding the night of the murders, Speck indulged freely in both of these habits, probably mixing drugs and alcohol, a potentially lethal combination.

Undoubtedly, there is a correlation between alcohol and murder, but this doesn't mean there is any causal connection. It can be a contributing factor, however. In her book, *Astrology of Alcoholism*, Ann Parker presents a statistical study of alcoholics in which the Moon or Ascendant in Virgo has a high rating. She also mentions some "alcohol prone" degrees (see the Appendix). Under this study, Speck's Virgo Ascendant would qualify, as would his Moon within the 9–11° Cancer range.

Chart 12, the event chart for Speck's forced entry into the nurses' dormitory, shows Aries rising with Mars in Cancer conjunct his natal Moon and square natal Mars, activating the aggressive and potentially violent Moon/Mars square in his natal chart. Because the police estimated that the time of Speck's entry was between 11:30 P.M. and midnight, this entry chart is erected for 11:33 P.M. CDT on July 13, 1966. In this chart, Mars exactly on the 4th house cusp squares the Ascendant at 3° Aries, denoting the vicious manner in which the murders were performed.

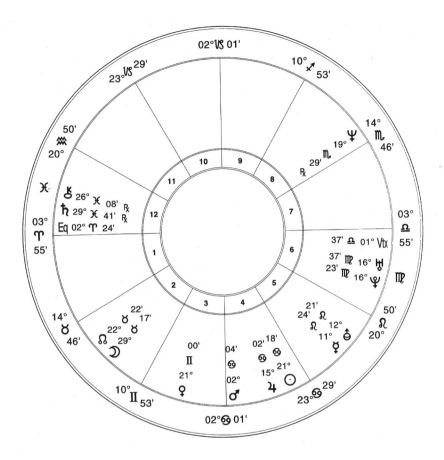

Chart 12. Event chart for Richard Speck's forced entry. July 13, 1966, 11:33 P.M. CDT, Chicago, IL, 87W39, 41N52. Placidus houses. Source: Time magazine article dated July 29, 1966.

The transiting Moon at 29° Taurus closely conjuncts Speck's natal Uranus and trines his natal Virgo Ascendant and Neptune, indicating the strange and mysterious manner in which the slayings occurred. The 25-26° area of Taurus, which the Moon occupies, marks the malefic fixed star, Caput Algol, which rules injury to the neck and throat, violent death, and beheading. The Pleiades, another malefic fixed star, which rules violent death, is located in the area of 27–29° Taurus, where Speck's natal Uranus is located. Speck's Saturn/Uranus conjunction is located between 23–27° Taurus, and is semi-square the Moon, which was at 10° Cancer.

Transiting Saturn at 29° Pisces is in exact opposition to Speck's natal Neptune and Ascendant degree, and occupies the 12th house of self-undoing in the event or horary chart for the forced entry. In Speck's natal chart Saturn rules the intercepted sign, Capricorn, on the cusp of his 4th house of endings; Saturn, the planet of karma and retribution, occupies the 8th house of his birth chart. Saturn's long transit and retrograde motion in the latter degrees of Pisces closely opposed Speck's natal Ascendant/Neptune conjunction at 29° Virgo and his prenatal eclipse at 27°48' Virgo throughout May, June, July, and August of 1966.

Speck claims he was so drugged that he recalls little or nothing of what happened after the murders, and his jail psychiatrist, Marvin Zipory, is inclined to believe him. In fact, Zipory stated that he believes Speck may have been "in a trance" on the night he killed the nurses.

Marvin Zipory was first assigned to Speck's case to determine whether or not the prisoner was still suicide-prone, and he interviewed Speck at two-week intervals while he was being held at the Cook County Jail. Zipory felt that Speck may have been the victim of considerable brain damage, and that the blackouts he claims to have experienced following the crime, and the frequent headaches he suffered, all point to this cause. Astrologically, Speck's natal Mars in the sign Aries (ruling the head) and afflicted by the Moon (ruling the brain and conscious mind) all suggest the possibility of this condition, and support Zipory's diagnosis. A panel of six doctors (five of whom were psychiatrists) examined Speck and declared him sane enough to stand trial. Zipory concurred with their opinions.

Speck's defense attorney, Gerald W. Getty, recommended that he plead "insanity," but when Speck refused to go along with this, a plea of "not guilty" was entered. Natal Saturn and Uranus in the sign Taurus (the Bull) indicates Speck's basic stubbornness—a trait he exercised in this instance. This Saturn/Uranus conjunction, falling as it does on or near the cusp of his 9th house (legal matters), trine his Ascendant (the self), also indicates the wide publicity the case received from the media. In fact, because of this wide publicity, the court was forced to hold the trial in Peoria, Illinois, instead of Chicago. Public Defender Getty, having introduced a plea of "not guilty," attempted to prove Speck was elsewhere at the time

Chart 13. Richard Speck's natal chart progressed to the murders on July 13, 1966. Born December 6, 1941, 1:00 A.M. CST, Kirkwood, IL, 90W45, 40N52. Placidus houses. Source: AFA Bulletin, February 19, 1985, Vol. 47, No. 2; birth certificate courtesy of Victoria Shaw.

of the crime. Two witnesses were produced to substantiate the alibi, but failed to convince the jury. The trial was held on February 20, 1967, and the jury, after deliberating forty-nine minutes, returned a verdict of "guilty." Speck was only twenty-four years old at the time of his conviction for murder in the first degree. Judge H. C. Paschen sentenced him in September 1967 to die in the electric chair, but after the United States Supreme Court's decision to eliminate capital punishment, Speck was re-sentenced to serve several life sentences, totaling more than four hundred years.

Chart 13 shows Speck's natal chart progressed to the date of the murders. Before analyzing these progressions, let's take a look at Speck's natal planets in relation to his childhood and parentage.

Speck spent his early childhood in Monmouth, Illinois, his adolescence in Dallas, Texas. The rulers of his 4th and 10th houses (denoting his parents) are in opposition (Mercury opposite Jupiter and the Moon semi-square Saturn), suggesting his parents were not closely in accord. Speck's father was a potter who died in 1946 when Speck was only six years old. At that age, Speck's progressed MC was inconjunct natal Mercury, his 10th house ruler, signifying the male parent. At birth, Speck's Mercury was trine Pluto.

The family moved to Dallas in 1950 when his mother remarried, providing him with a stepfather whom he gradually grew to despise.(Natal Sun in Sagittarius is often an indicator of a stepparent, although this is not invariably so.) Because his stepfather was handicapped, he was obliged to repress the expression of his resentment to some degree. Speck's mother stated in an interview that her new husband not only failed to establish a good relationship with Speck, but actually harassed him unmercifully. By contrast, Speck's relationship with his mother was much better. Jupiter, ruler of Speck's 4th house (representing the mother), is elevated near the Midheaven, and this planet at 16° Gemini is also the dispositor of Speck's natal Sun sign, Sagittarius. Jupiter opposes Speck's natal Sun at 13° Sagittarius. His natal Moon, ruling the mother, is strong and at home in Cancer in the 10th house. Speck is said to have held his mother in high esteem, befitting this placement.

Speck was one of eight children, and was said to be especially fond of his younger sister, Carolyn. Note the trine of Mars to the Sun and Mercury in Sagittarius in the 3rd house, which rules siblings. Pluto rules the 3rd house, and this planet opposes Venus. Speck had two brothers and five sisters. His relatives claim that although he was occasionally violent when he was drinking heavily, most of the time he was tender, loving, and kind, especially to members of his own family circle.

Nevertheless, by age eighteen, Speck was completely out of control, and eventually was institutionalized in a juvenile home. this is a common pattern; murderers of multiple victims often begin their violent careers at an early age. The process usually begins in childhood and continues into adolescence. Sometimes it begins with cruelty to animals and/or arson, and develops into assault, voyeurism, and rape. Then, the violence accelerates into a rage that often ends in murder, or occasionally suicide. Unfortunately, murder and suicide are often interrelated.

As an adult, Speck couldn't seem to hold down a steady job. He dropped out of school in the ninth grade and worked as a garbage hauler and a trucker's helper, and held temporary seafaring jobs. Dreamy Neptune ruling his 6th house (jobs) didn't help a bit. In fact, between dead-end, low-paying jobs he was often arrested for theft (Mercury) or breaking and entering, ending up in jail. When arrested on July 17, 1966 for the massacre in Chicago, Speck was also wanted for burglary in Dallas, Texas. In his natal chart, Mercury, his ruler, trines Pluto (gangsters, convicts) in the 11th house, indicating that he chose the wrong companions.

No doubt, these factors and his heavy drinking adversely affected his marriage. In Speck's natal chart, Venus sextiles Mercury, his Ascendant ruler. This aspect points to his attraction to a young (Mercury) girl, for Speck's wife was only fifteen years old when they married in January 1962. They had a daughter of whom he was very fond (see Venus on the cusp of his 5th house of progeny).

Neptune, Speck's 7th house ruler, is exactly opposite the Descendent and poorly aspected except for a trine to Uranus and Saturn. Speck's wife, Shirley, filed for divorce while he was in prison and won permanent custody of their only daughter (Uranus in the 9th house of legalities trine Neptune). Undoubtedly, this marital failure affected him strongly and negatively colored his attitude toward women in general. His hatred for his former wife became an obsession. Neptune in Virgo, poorly aspected, often leads to self-pity, or "playing the martyr." The loss of his child became progressively harder to bear, especially when his ex-wife remarried shortly after their divorce. Moon in Cancer gives a moody, brooding, oversensitive nature, and Jupiter square the Nodes across the 6th and 12th houses tends to magnify things and blow them all out of proportion.

Speck's natal Sun and Moon are in inconjunct aspect; at the time of the murders on July 13, 1966, his progressed Moon and progressed Sun repeat this inconjunct aspect. Progressed Mars, a violent planet, at 24° Aries is on the cusp of his 8th house, which rules sexuality, and is exactly square his progressed MC at 24° Cancer. At age twenty-four, progressed Jupiter, Speck's Sun sign ruler, had retrograded to an exact opposition of his natal Sun, indicating the potential for self-indulgence and excessive pleasure-seeking. With Jupiter square the natal Moon's Nodes at his birth, he was inclined to be a braggart who seldom felt the need to be truthful.

Epilogue

On December 5, 1991, the day of his annual solar return, and just one day before his fiftieth birthday, Speck died of a massive heart attack. He died in Silver Cross Hospital near the Joliet, Illinois, prison where he had been held for twenty-four years. On the day of his death, the New Moon at 13°42' Sagittarius fell exactly on his natal Sun's degree and opposed his 4th house ruler, his progressed Sun at 4° Aquarius opposed natal Pluto at 5° Leo; the progressed Moon at 16° Taurus occupying his 8th house was semisextile natal Jupiter, ruler of his 4th house of endings.

AP/ Wide World Photos

Chapter Four

The Assassination of John Lennon

On December 8, 1980, former Beatle John Lennon and his wife Yoko Ono were preparing to enter their Manhattan apartment when Mark David Chapman approached them. He called out to Lennon, then leveled a pistol and shot five times.

Lennon staggered about five feet, shouting "I've been shot," before he collapsed to the sidewalk. Upon arrival at the hospital, John Lennon was pronounced dead.

Chapman made no attempt to escape, was arrested and immediately confined to Bellevue Hospital in Manhattan to ascertain his sanity and ability to stand trial for Lennon's murder. He was pronounced fit, arraigned, and charged with second degree murder. Chapman had a history of previous arrests from 1972 to 1980. The latest was an armed robbery charge that occurred less than two months before the shooting,

Beatle fans know John Lennon as the composer and singer of many popular hit songs during the '60s and '70s. He was shot and killed by a man who had an acute identity problem: a man who believed *he* was John Lennon and that the real John Lennon was usurping his own position and deceiving the public about his true identity. This is according to the psychiatrist who examined Chapman prior to the trial. Twenty-five years old at the time of the shootings, Chapman had reportedly sought help from a counselor at a mental health clinic in Honolulu, Hawaii, just three weeks prior to the shootings, but failed to keep his appointment. According to friends, he was a former drug user and a "born again Christian" who had married young, and was experiencing relationship problems. Before coming to New York City, Chapman held a job as a security guard in Waikiki (where he purchased the murder weapon), but had hastily resigned without explanation, signing himself out under the name "John Lennon."

According to Rodden's *Astro Data III*, Mark David Chapman was born May 10, 1955, in Fort Worth, Texas, at 7:30 P.M. CST, when a Jupiter/Uranus conjunction in Cancer squared Neptune in 26° Libra; see Chart 14. An afflicted Neptune suggests a confused mental state (identity confusion), possibly aggravated by drugs or alcohol. In this case, if we are to believe the psychiatrist, "displaced identity" was the result. For several months now, transiting Pluto in the last decan of Libra had been hovering around Chapman's natal Neptune, making a hard square aspect to his Jupiter/Uranus conjunction in 24° Cancer, and conjoining his natal Neptune. These intense aspects indicate the need to escape (Neptune) from growing inner tensions by seeking some type of psychotherapy (Pluto), but unfortunately he aborted his own attempt to do so.

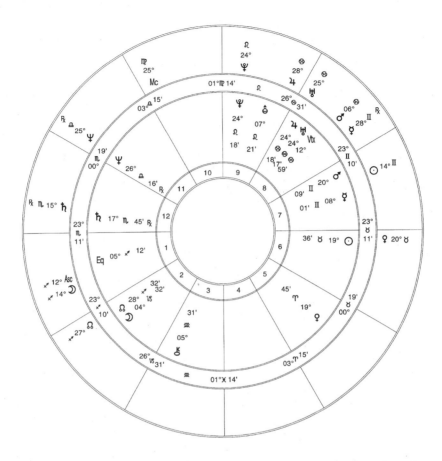

Chart 14. Natal chart for Mark David Chapman, progressed to John Lennon's murder on December 8, 1980. Born: May 10, 1955, 7:30 P.M. CST, Fort Worth, TX, 97W18, 32N45 Source: Lois Rodden's Astro Data 111, page 43. ("AA" data, D. Martinie, from a private source.)

Chapman's birth chart shows the Moon's Nodes on the Gemini/Sagittarius axis favorably aspecting his Taurus Sun sign ruler, Venus, confirming and emphasizing his religious zeal. Mars in Gemini conjunct the South Node and sextile Venus, clearly indicates a devout, enthusiastic missionary type who readily adopts a cause and enjoys traveling to foreign countries. A Yod configuration (often called "The Finger of God") appears on the angles of his birth chart. Venus and Mars are in sextile aspect, while Saturn, the focal planet of the Yod, is inconjunct both planets.

Mars and Pluto are the co-rulers of Chapman's 23° Scorpio Ascendant, and both planets are strong and angular. Chapman's Pluto at 24° Leo is culminating at the zenith ,and closely squares his Ascendant. His Sun at 19° Taurus opposes restrictive Saturn, and Pluto is in a tension-promoting square aspect to both planets; a T-Cross in fixed signs. Sun square Pluto hints at a volatile, vindicative nature if crossed (potential violence), while the Sun opposite Saturn suggests that he suffers from low self-esteem, accompanied by feelings of insecurity and periodic bouts of depression (Saturn). Although in the 12th house, Saturn is within a six degree orb, and therefore aspecting the Ascendant.

On the night of the murder, Lennon's progressed Uranus at 24° Taurus trines Chapman's progressed MC, and opposes Chapman's Scorpio Ascendant, bringing the two of them together in a violent confrontation! Chapman's ruling planet, Pluto, exactly squares Lennon's progressed Uranus, and his natal Venus at 19° Aries is exactly conjunct Lennon's ascendant degree. (Venus is not such a lucky planet this time, as Chapman posed as a friend to gain access to Lennon.) Lennon's progressed Sun at 26° Scorpio opposes his own natal Uranus, thereby increasing his potential for incurring risky (Uranus) encounters, situations, and/or accidents.

According to Lois Rodden's Data News, John Winston Lennon was born to Julia and Fred Lennon in a Liverpool (England) hospital during a bombing raid on October 9, 1940 at 6:30 P.M.. BST. (Refer to author's note at the end of this chapter; see Chart 15.).

Let's examine Lennon's birth chart closely. The 19th degree of Aries, a Mars-ruled fire sign is rising. Lennon has a stellium of points and planets in the artistic, fun-loving sign of Libra. and his Sun in the 16th degree of this cardinal sign occupies a musical degree. (Fifteen degrees of the Cardinal signs, according to astrologer Charles Carter, denotes musical talent.) The Moon's node in the harmonious sign of Libra conjunct his natal Sun accounts for much of his personal charm and immense popularity. Having an angular Sun at birth (near the Descendant) he was instinctively drawn to an occupation dealing with the public, so he became a very successful musician and entertainer. The stellium of Taurus planets in his 1st house and the sign Taurus on his 2nd cusp signifies the accumulation of great wealth and abundant material possessions.

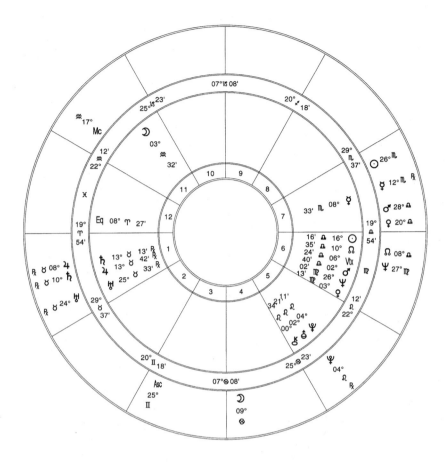

Chart 15. *John Lennon's birth chart, progressed to his death on December 8, 1980. Born October 9, 1940, 6:30 P.M. BST, Liverpool, England, 2W55, 53N25. Placidus Houses. Source: Lois Rodden's Data News. ("A" data, Charles Harvey, from Lennon's relatives.)*

His setting Sun opposes the Ascendant, however, showing the abrupt separation from his father. As a little boy he was left to live with his grandparents (represented by the Jupiter/Saturn conjunction in his 1st house), but was actually raised by an aunt. At age 17, when Lenon's progressed Sun squared his natal Moon and Pluto, his mother Julia died in a tragic automobile accident. Note that Lennon's Moon (the mother) at birth at 3° Aquarius is applying to an opposition to Pluto in 4° Leo, an unfortunate and potentially violent aspect.

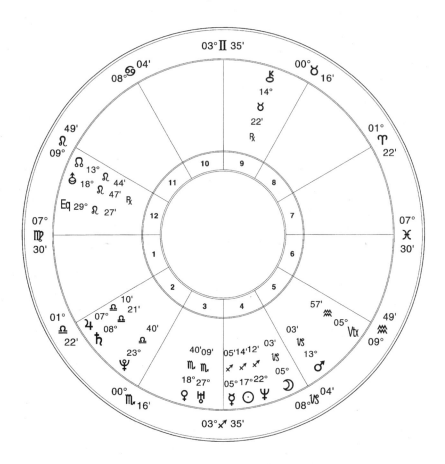

Chart 16. Event chart for John Lennon's shooting. December 8, 1980, 10:50 P.M. EST, Manhattan, NY, 73W59, 40N46. Source: Baton Rouge Morning Advocate newspaper.

Cancer/Capricorn falls across Lennon's natal 4th and 10th house axis. Moon-ruled Cancer is known to rule New York City, where he made his home at the time of his death. Ironically, the former Beatle had said he felt safe in New York City because it provided more privacy than Liverpool, his home town.

When Lennon met his violent death at 10:50 P.M. EST, on December 8, 1980 (see Chart 16), his progressed Moon was at exactly 9°52' of Cancer near the cusp of his 4th house of endings and squaring the Nodes. The transiting Moon was in his 10th house in Capricorn, which is the sign it occupied at Chapman's birth. The Moon's first aspect on that day was a square to Lennon's natal Mars, then the Moon made a trine to Venus, and finally a fatal inconjunct aspect to natal Transpluto and Pluto, activating his natal Mars/Pluto midpoint. Lennon's natal Mars/Pluto midpoint (murder) is at 3°16' Virgo, and on the date of his birth, his Sun sign ruler, Venus, at 3° Virgo is conjunct this midpoint, making what Uranian astrologers call a "tree" or occupied midpoint.

Venus also rules his 7th house, no doubt representing the presence of his devoted wife, Yoko Ono, as a witness to his murder. At the time of the shootings, the transiting Moon at 5° Capricorn is in exact opposition to Yoko Ono's progressed Vertex at 5° Cancer. The transiting Moon conjuncts Chapman's natal Moon and prenatal eclipse point of "fated encounters" at 2°59' Capricorn. The Moon is also making a stressful sesquiquadrate to Chapman's natal Sun and progressed Venus.

Let's examine event Chart 16 for the murder more closely to see what aspects some of the other transiting planets made to Lennon's natal chart. At birth, Lennon had an exact Jupiter/Saturn conjunction at 13° Taurus in his 1st house. On the date of his death, this conjunction was squared by the Moon's Nodes at 13° Leo/Aquarius. Transiting Mars was exactly trine this natal Jupiter/Saturn conjunction. Mars at 13° Capricorn in Lennon's 10th house squared his natal Ascendant, Sun, Moon's Nodes, and Equatorial Ascendant. Saturn, his 10th house ruler, at 8° Libra was conjunct his progressed North Node, as well as his wife's natal Ascendant. Transiting Mercury, representing cars and transportation, at 5° Sagittarius (ruler of Lennon's 3rd house of short trips), was making a separating trine aspect to his natal Pluto when he was shot and killed just as he and his wife stepped out of their limousine. Mercury squares Pluto at his birth.

Let's look at the transits of the slower-moving outer planets to Lennon's birth chart for the date of his assassination. Transiting Pluto at 23° Libra in his 7th house opposes Lennon's Ascendant and conjuncts his Libra Sun, and is approaching a conjunction with progressed Mars at 28° Libra. Transiting Uranus, which acts quickly and unexpectedly, was at 27° Scorpio, making a conjunction to Lennon's progressed Sun.

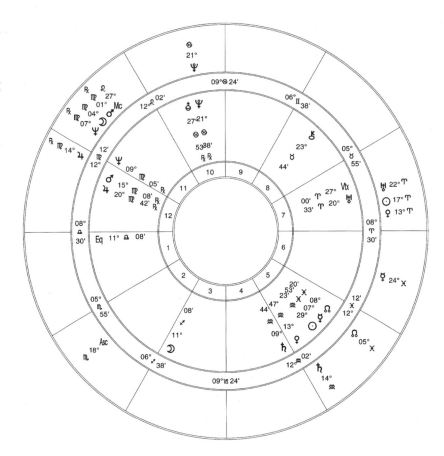

Chart 17. Birth chart for Yoko Ono, progressed to December 8, 1980. Born February 18, 1933, 8:30 P.M. JST, Tokyo, Japan, 139E45, 35N40. Placidus houses. Source: Birth certificate supplied by Roger Elliot to Lois Rodden; published in Profiles of Women, *pg. 333.*

Lennon met his death a few days before the exact conjunction of Jupiter and Saturn at 9° Libra. This conjunction fell in opposition to Lennon's 8° Aries Equatorial Ascendant and conjunct his prenatal eclipse point (PE) at 8°11' Libra. In her book on the prenatal eclipse, astrologer Rose Lineman associates this eclipse point with karmic relationships and debts.

The alignment of two of the largest planets in our solar system, Jupiter and Saturn, takes place every twenty years. A Jupiter/Saturn conjunction in Earth sign Capricorn took place on December 31, 1980, 23 days after

Lennon's death. If we apply it to Lennon's birth chart, we see that it falls within his overloaded 6th house, conjunct his progressed North Node. When Lennon was born in 1940, Jupiter and Saturn were also forming an Earth sign conjunction, this time at 13° Taurus, in Lennon's 1st house.

Now, let's return to Lennon's natal chart. At birth, Uranus makes a stressful sesquiquadrate to the Moon's Nodes. In 1980, transiting Uranus at 27° Scorpio was just barely past the exact opposition to Lennon's natal Uranus at 25° Taurus. This middle-age crisis point is especially important as it frequently represents a turning point in one's life. Not necessarily a violent change, but a change in values and sometimes lifestyle. Males, especially, can experience a sexual crisis at this age.

Lennon's biographers tend to agree that he did, indeed, experience such a Uranian crisis or sudden change in life-style. Yoko Ono and John Lennon were married on March 20, 1969. But throughout 1973 and 1974 when transiting Uranus was conjunct his natal Sun, he lived apart from his Japanese wife and reportedly had an affair with his secretary which lasted about eighteen months. He later reconciled with with his estranged wife, and in 1976 their son Sean was born on Lennon's birthday. Shortly afterward, he switched roles with his wife and began to stay at home to care for his young son, while Yoko became more active in her own career, and took over the management of their business affairs. In 1980, Lennon and his wife, having come full circle, began making musical albums together again.

Yoko Ono's birth data is derived from *Rodden's Profiles of Women*, and is said to be "A" data from her birth certificate. She was born on February 18, 1933, 8:30 P.M. JST, in Tokyo, Japan; see Chart 17.

Both Chapman and Lennon, by some strange quirk of fate, were married to women of a different culture. Chapman's wife was Japanese-American while Lennon's wife was Japanese. Lennon's natal Pluto in Leo in aspect to Mars and Venus shows he might be attracted to a woman of a different race or country. Individuals having Pluto in the 5th or 7th house at birth, or in the signs Leo or Libra, often make interracial or intercultural marriages. Pluto here indicates the extra adjustment it takes to make this type of marriage succeed.

Epilogue

Mark David Chapman has been sentenced to life imprisonment, and is now confined to a prison cell in New York's Attica Correctional Facility. Chapman's record shows he was mentally ill and unstable during much of his lifetime, and it is alleged that he attempted suicide in 1977 when he was 22 years old.

Author's Note

I, along with many other astrologers, have previously used 7:00 A.M. BST as Lennon's birth time, using Hunter Davies' biography *The Beatles* as a reference. Now, however, it seems there is more reliable data available. The 6:30 P.M. time of birth utilized in this book is now used by most astrologers, including the British astrologer, A.T. Mann, in his book *Life Time Astrology*, in which he analyzes Lennon's chart at great length. I now favor the 6:30 P.M. BST birth time because, after analyzing it thoroughly, I believe it fits more accurately with the somewhat turbulent events in John Lennon's short but active life.

AP/ Wide World Photos

Chapter Five

Murder Unmasked

The Many Faces of Ted Bundy

"What's one less person on the face of the earth, anyway?" These were Ted Bundy's reported words when referring to himself just before his scheduled execution on July 2, 1986. The execution was postponed, but after ten years of appealing his convictions for multiple murders, Bundy died in the electric chair in 1989.

A cold-blooded serial killer, Bundy was convicted of three vicious slayings of young women in Florida on July 24, 1979, and was suspected by police of killing as many as thirty-six women in Washington, Oregon, Utah, and Colorado. After being imprisoned in Colorado for abducting Carol Da Ronch, he escaped twice, avoiding detection by the police through his mastery of the art of disguise (Neptune) and his amazing ability to move with speed from place to place (natal Mars conjunct Moon in Sagittarius opposite Uranus in Gemini).

At the time of Bundy's birth (See Chart 18) in Burlington, Vermont, on November 24, 1946, at 10:35 P.M. EST, the Sun, his Leo Ascendant ruler, occupied 2° Sagittarius. This "A" data is said to be from the birth certificate, according to Rodden's *Astro Data III*. Bundy was born the day after a New Moon (November 23) and a solar eclipse at 0°50' Sagittarius; this prenatal eclipse fell in his 4th house. The Moon is in its increasing or extrovert phase. The 25th degree of Leo rises and 16° Taurus is on the Midheaven. Both degrees denote "a homicidal tendency" according to Charles Carter's *Encyclopedia of Psychological Astrology*. Bundy's Moon in the 17th degree of Sagittarius is also "a homicidal degree," according to the same source, and its conjunction to Mars and opposition to Uranus only adds to the potential for violence directed at females (Moon).

Many of Bundy's acquaintances noticed his remarkable ability to alter his appearance, seemingly at will. He was a chameleon, a changeling, adept at disguises and mimicry. Six mug shots taken of him and displayed in national newspapers seem to reveal a set of different personalities. Having studied law, a Sagittarian occupation, it was easy for Bundy to pose as a newly enrolled law student on college campuses. Mars, ruler of his 9th house of legal matters, is conjunct his Sun in Sagittarius. With Neptune (disguises and deceptions) exactly semisquare his Leo Ascendant and natal Mercury, he also enjoyed using various names and aliases in his efforts to elude and outwit the police.

His good looks and charming, polite demeanor (Sun sextile Neptune) appealed to vulnerable women. His surface charm and grace were combined with the athletic, dignified bearing typical of Leo rising. To lure

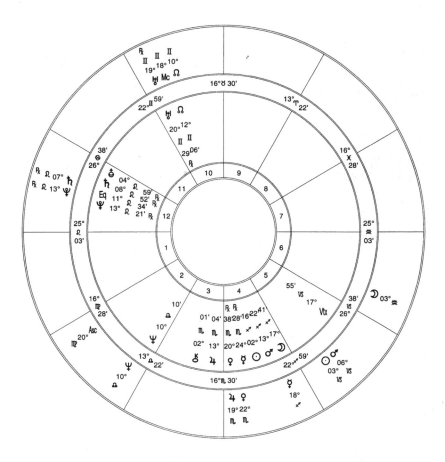

Chart 18. Birth chart for Ted Bundy, progressed to Chi Omega murders on January 15, 1978. Born November 24, 1946, 10:35 P.M. EST, Burlington, VT, 73W12, 44N29. Source: T. Pat Davis, quoting Bundy's birth certificate published in Lois Rodden's Astro Data 111, page 34.

women and evoke sympathy, he occasionally posed as a cripple or wore his arm in a sling. His appearance varied. Sometimes he wore his hair short, sometimes long. At times he had a mustache or beard, at other times he was clean-shaven. This was his way of evading the police, for as soon as he was in trouble in one place, he'd move to another state to begin again with a new name and fraudulent ID and credit cards. It worked for a while, but the police finally caught up with him. After escaping jail in California, he was arrested in Florida on February 15, 1978, attempting to leave the state in a stolen Volkswagen.

As soon as his true identity was discovered, the state of Utah wanted him back to serve a kidnapping sentence, and Colorado wanted to try him for murder, as well as two prison breaks; but Florida had plans to try him for the brutal Chi Omega sorority house murders. On January 15, 1978, four young co-eds had been bludgeoned with a club and viciously raped by an intruder. Two died immediately. The two who survived the attack were later called as witnesses in Bundy's 1979 trial.

Bundy was thirty-two years old when he was tried in Miami, Florida, for the Chi Omega murders. He was convicted at 9:00 P.M. EDT on July 24, 1979. See Chart 19 for transits on that date.

Chart 18 shows Bundy's natal chart and progressions for January 15, 1978—the date of the Chi Omega sorority house murders. Bundy's progressed Midheaven had moved to 18°08' Gemini, opposite progressed Mercury at 18°18' Sagittarius and conjunct progressed Uranus at 19° Gemini, signifying the legalities that would ultimately lead to his loss of freedom. When transiting Mars at 20° Gemini conjoined both his progressed Midheaven and natal Uranus, law-breaking brought about a sudden crisis in his life. By 1979, when he was convicted, his progressed Ascendant at 21° Virgo was moving away from a square to Uranus and making a favorable sextile to his natal Venus, so his family stood by him and even offered to pay his legal expenses.

Neptune conjunct his natal Moon fostered unrealistic hopes of evading punishment, and Bundy gained his mother's complete loyalty and sympathy. She pleaded for his life on the witness stand, but transiting Saturn (the Reaper) square his natal Moon's Node/Mars conjunction wasn't about to let him escape so easily this time, and exacted just and final retribution. The progressed Moon square progressed Venus and transiting Uranus at 16° Scorpio, exactly opposite the cusp of his 10th house (reputation) describes the loss of prestige he suffered, as well as the sudden (Uranus angular) notoriety he gained through extensive media coverage when his trial was nationally televised.

Bundy fired his attorneys during the course of the trial, and defended himself. The case against him was too strong to overcome, though, and a guilty verdict was rendered on July 24, 1979. Bundy was sentenced on July 31 and subsequently sent to Death Row at the Florida State Prison

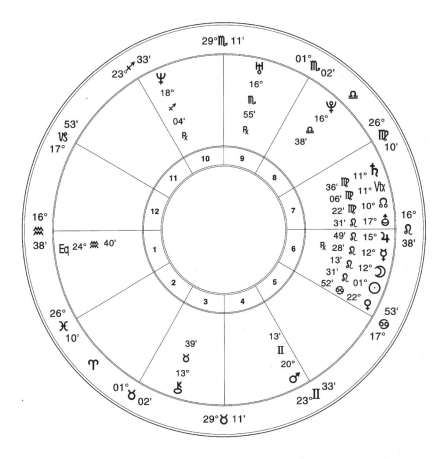

*Chart 19. Event chart for Ted Bundy's conviction for the Chi Omega sorority murders.
July 24, 1979, 9:00 P.M. EDT, Miami, FL, 80W11, 25N47. Placidus houses. Source:
Stephen Michaud and Hugh Aynesworth's book* The Only Living Witness, *page 271.*

to await execution. As a result of constant appeals by his attorneys during the following ten years, he managed to postpone the inevitable, but he
was finally executed on January 24, 1989, at 7:06 A.M. EST, in Starke,
Florida. He was pronounced dead at 7:16 A.M. See Chart 20. Note how
the vertical angles of his birth chart are reversed in the death chart, so that
the natal 4th house angle becomes the MC at the time of his public execution. On this date, transiting Pluto at 15° Scorpio was square natal Pluto, and just 1 degree from a conjunction to his natal 4th house cusp at

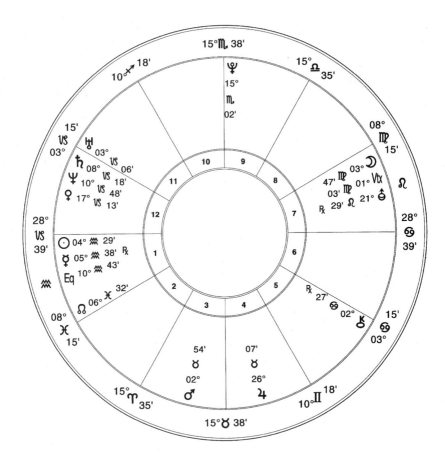

Chart 20. Event chart for Ted Bundy's death by electrocution. January 24, 1989, 7:06 A.M. EST, Starke, FL, 82W07, 29N57. Source: American Astrology *magazine, May 1989, page 18.*

16°30' Scorpio. Pluto rules his 4th house, representing the end of life.

Does Bundy's childhood and parentage, as depicted by the natal Moon's aspects, give us a clue to the motivation behind his criminal activities? Does Neptune semisquare Mercury in Scorpio in the 4th house (heritage) point to his mother's well-kept secret about his father? Ted Bundy didn't know he was an illegitimate child. When he was thirteen, he found his birth certificate with the words "father unknown" hidden among some old papers. Until then, he'd mistakenly believed his father was dead. His mother had evidently had a love affair with a serviceman who abandoned her when he learned she was pregnant She had no choice but to go to a home for unwed mothers in Burlington, Vermont. Her son, Theodore Robert Cowell, was born there on November 24, 1946. He would be told by his grandparents that his mother was his sister.

In 1950, at age four, Bundy's progressed Midheaven at 20° Taurus opposed his natal 10th house ruler, Venus. His mother, Louise, then married John Bundy, by whom she had four children. When questioned about these early years, Bundy recalled only that he resented being uprooted from his grandparent's home. Louise's father, Sam Cowell, was a church deacon, and the child sorely missed him when the two families moved apart. His relationship with his stepfather suffered by comparison.

Further examination of Bundy's birth chart shows the 4th house cusp (Scorpio), ruling the mother, is strongly emphasized; with five planets clustered within a thirty-four degree space in this house. The ruler, Pluto, at 13° Leo, is conjunct Saturn at 8° Leo in the 12th house of secrets and behind-the-scenes activity. Pluto conjunct Saturn indicates he may have suffered from lack of a strong parental father-image during his growing years. Venus square Pluto describes the secrecy surrounding his parents' relationship and how it may have affected him, since these two planets rule his parental angles—the 4th and 10th houses. His natal Mercury semisquare Neptune (lies and deception) shows how this secrecy may have affected him in an adverse manner.

Bundy directed his violent impulses toward females rather than males. There's no recorded incident indicating otherwise. If he was angry with his mother upon learning about the circumstances surrounding his birth (Moon conjunct Mars), he likely failed to confront his true feelings, repressing his anger. Natal Moon opposite Uranus indicates deep-seated estrangement from the mother, which later influenced the stability of his relationships with other women. Mars opposite Uranus suggests that his discovery of his illegitimate birth may have triggered a shock that was more important than he was willing to acknowledge.

The 3rd house (siblings) and the 10th house (the father) are both ruled by Venus, which is heavily afflicted, despite its conjunction to Jupiter. Venus inconjunct Uranus suggests unconventional or abnormal sexual desires, and Venus square Pluto makes him subject to peculiar phobias and obsessions. Venus was retrograde and in its detriment in the sign of Scorpio at Bundy's birth, but turned direct by progression the year after he learned of his illegitimate birth. Venus' station at that time, as Bundy reached adolescence, marked an important turning point in his life.

A retrograde Venus can indicate sexual deviation if it's heavily afflicted in a male chart, according to Manik C. Jain, author of *Astrology in Marriage Counseling*. In a chapter on sexual perversion and aversion, he states that "men who molest women and are subject to dangerous and vicious acts against the opposite sex, often have Venus retrograde and heavily afflicted at birth."

Let's take a closer look at Bundy's natal chart. An exact trine between Mars at 13° Sagittarius and Pluto in 13° Leo denotes potential violence, and this aspect is often a contributing factor of satyriasis—uncontrollable sexual desire. Mars and Pluto are co-rulers of the 8th sign, Scorpio, which occupies his death-related 4th house cusp. According to the precepts of Cosmobiology in Ebertin's *Combination of Stellar Influences*, the negative side of the Mars/Pluto midpoint signifies murder and brutality. Bundy's natal Neptune (his 8th house ruler of sexuality) located at this midpoint denotes "a tendency to cause harm to others secretly and unobtrusively."

Psychiatrists who analyzed Bundy in prison labeled him a sociopathic personality. From their interviews, we also know some other interesting facts about him:

- His IQ was estimated at 124;
- He had an O-Positive blood type;
- He was left-handed;
- He had an almost obsessive love for Volkswagens;
- He was suspected of having a foot fetish, as demonstrated by the fact that when arrested he owned over forty pairs of socks;
- His victims were either strangled with panty hose or bludgeoned to death—when questioned about this, Bundy remarked that a club was "probably" chosen because the weapon couldn't be traced;
- When speaking of the murders, he avoided referring to himself directly and invariably used the third person.

Despite his craving for publicity (typical of the Leo Ascendant), and his cooperation with reporters and writers who agreed to relate his story, Bundy made no official confession. Throughout his imprisonment, he denied any feelings of guilt and proclaimed his innocence of the Chi Omega murders, despite his conviction in 1979 (though he finally did confess to twenty-three murders in the Pacific Northwest). But Mercury square the natal Ascendant made him verbose and willing to enter into discussions about the crimes, his trial, and other related events, so he was frequently open to interviews with reporters until the date of his execution.

As a result, several books have been published about Ted Bundy. Many facts about his life, alleged crimes, and some important chronological events can be found in *The Only Living Witness*, Bundy's own story told in the third person. It is based on taped interviews with Bundy in prison and written by reporters G. Michaud and Hugh Aynesworth. *Bundy, The Deliberate Stranger* by Richard W. Larsen is another interesting factual account about Bundy.

The Stranger Beside Me, by Ann Rule, is written by a former police-woman who worked with Bundy at a Washington suicide crisis center. She was not only personally acquainted with him, but also carried on a friendly correspondence with him after his imprisonment. The female viewpoint is also expressed in *The Phantom Prince*, written by Meg Anders, about a woman who had a love affair with Bundy for several years when he resided in Utah. They planned to marry, but never did. In June of 1977, Bundy learned that she was contemplating marriage to another man.

Throughout his trials and subsequent convictions, Bundy never lacked female supporters. While imprisoned, awaiting trial, he befriended Carole Boone. Just two days after his conviction for the brutal murder of twelve-year-old Kimberly Leach, Ted Bundy and Carole Boone were married. Their unusual marriage took place during the Kimberly murder trial at 10:13 A.M. EST, on February 9, 1980, in Orlando, Florida. At the time, his progressed Moon had reached 28°53' Aquarius, just three degrees within his 7th house cusp. See Chart 21 for transits on the wedding date. Carole Boone had Bundy's child in October 1980.

Other progressions and transits for these two closely related events are as follows: Progressed Midheaven at 20° Gemini exactly conjunct his 7th

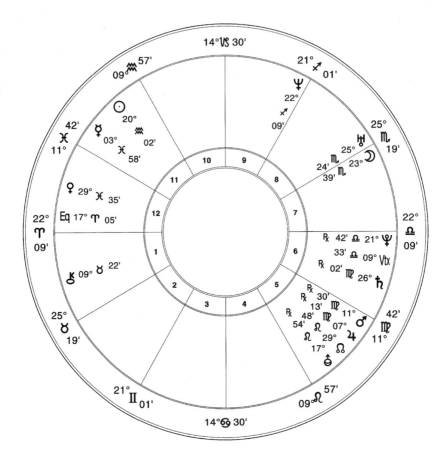

Chart 21. Event chart for Ted Bundy's marriage (while imprisoned) to Carole Boone. February 9, 1980, 10:13 A.M. EST, Orlando, FL 81W23, 28N33. Placidus houses. Source: Stephen Michaud and Hugh Aynesworth's book The Only Living Witness, page 290.

house ruler, Uranus, and inconjunct Venus; progressed Mercury conjunct the 5th house of courtship and children, and progressed Venus at 24° Scorpio conjunct Uranus at 25° Scorpio square his 7th house cusp at 24° Aquarius; progressed Mars at 8° Capricorn is inconjunct Saturn, coruler of the 7th house of marriage.

By his own admission, Bundy's violent, murderous impulses began to dominate his life beginning in 1972 when he was twenty-six years old. His criminal career started with minor thefts and voyeurism, and progressed into a tragic pattern of molesting and finally murdering young women. He especially liked to victimize pretty young women who wore their hair long and parted in the middle.

On his twenty-sixth birthday, Bundy's progressed Midheaven had reached 12°55' Gemini and begun its opposition to his natal Mars/South Node conjunction at 12 and 13° Sagittarius. His natal 4th house stellium is probably one of the worst aspects in his entire chart. Mars is conjunct both luminaries and occupies the Sun/Moon midpoint, increasing his potential for aggressive, impulsive behavior. When unleashed, Bundy's predatory hatred for women knew no bounds, as indicated by his afflicted Moon (females) conjunct Mars (violence)and the South Node. This dangerous feature indicates a great potential for uncontrolled aggression directed primarily at women.

It's believed that Bundy's first victim was eighteen-year-old Mary Adams, who was battered in the basement of her Seattle, Washington, home on January 4, 1974. There may have been previous victims whose bodies were never found. Bundy was twenty-seven in January 1974 when the crime against Mary Adams was reported. His retrograde, progressed Venus had recently returned to the same position it held at birth. Two months later, in March 1974, his progressed Moon also returned to its natal position.

Thus began five years of kidnapping, molesting, and murdering women. This horrifying behavior continued from 1974 to 1979, when his progressed Midheaven reached a conjunction with Uranus and he was finally convicted and sent to prison. Saturn conjunct Pluto in his 12th house of confinement and karmic retribution had pulled the plug on him.

Epilogue

Bundy earned a Bachelor of Science degree in psychology and held several jobs relating to social work and politics. He held a staff position in 1972 for the Republican Party, and once had a job answering a suicide hotline. When he was arrested on July 24, 1979, for the rape and murder of two co-eds from the Chi Omega sorority, he was posing as a law student at a college in Florida. On July 31, 1979, Ted Bundy received two death sentences and two life imprisonment sentences; at this time his progressed Moon had reached 22° Aquarius. He received a third death sentence on

February 12, 1980, when his progressed Moon was at 28°59' Aquarius. When Bundy's last appeal was rejected on January 17th, 1989, Florida Governor Martinez signed a fourth death warrant.

Shortly before his execution on January 24, 1989, Bundy finally confessed to twenty-three murders in the northwestern states. On September 11, 1988, just four months before his execution by electrocution, there was a solar eclipse at 18°40' Virgo, closely squaring his natal Uranus and natal Moon in the 4th house of endings.

Reporters Stephen G. Michaud and Hugh Aynesworth recorded some of his last words in *Ted Bundy: Conversations with a Killer*, published in 1990. In one last taped interview with Dr. James Dobson of Pomona, California, Bundy stated that he wasn't an abused or neglected child and that his family was not to blame for his crimes, as he was raised in a Christian home. He also stated that he had discovered pornography (Neptune) when he was about twelve, and blamed this for the beginning of his moral and ethical downfall.

AP/ Wide World Photos

Chapter Six

The Last Ride

A Hitchhiker Who Was Almost Murdered

Fifteen-year-old Mary Bell Vincent had big plans when she ran away from her Las Vegas home, and a family of six brothers and sisters. She dreamed of making it in California, of becoming a movie star. Looking slightly older than her age, she was blessed with photogenic good looks. Mary Bell moved in with her twenty-six-year-old boyfriend in Marin County near San Francisco, but had to make other plans when he was arrested. She desperately wanted to go to the Los Angeles area, and to the nearby little town of Corona where her grandfather lived.

Despite warnings she'd received about the dangers of hitchhiking, Mary Bell decided to take the risk and attempt to hitch a ride to Los Angeles. On September 29, 1978, at about 3:00 P.M. PDT, Lawrence Singleton, in his blue van, picked Mary Bell up just outside of Berkeley; see Chart 22. Larry, a fifty-one-year-old former merchant seaman, told her he had a daughter her age and promised to take her to the Interstate highway. Instead, he drove her to a deserted rural area where he raped her, chopped her arms off below the elbows with an ax, and drove away, leaving her to bleed to death. Despite the overwhelming odds against her, she managed to survive and identify her assailant.

In Galt, California, at about 8:00 A.M. PDT the following day, September 30, 1978, Mary Bell crawled through the brush to the highway, and holding her arms over her head to control the bleeding, attempted to stop a driver. One car passed by, then another. Finally, a couple of vacationers in the third car stopped to rescue her. Naked, and weak from loss of blood, she was taken to a hospital by Mr. and Mrs. Dennis Bor. See Chart 23 for transits at the time of the rescue.

Ten days later, on October 9, 1978, at 12:01 P.M. PDT, Singleton was arrested at his second wife's home in Sparks, Nevada; see Chart 24. Transiting Sun and Pluto were conjunct at 16° Libra, squaring his natal Pluto and Mercury in Cancer, and semisquare his natal Mars and Saturn. The Moon opposed his natal Mercury. He offered no resistance when the police arrested him, and pleaded not guilty to the charges.

Larry Singleton was born on July 28, 1927, in Tampa, Florida. His time of birth is unknown, so we'll erect a sunrise chart for 5:53:37 A.M. EST, since this is the actual time of sunrise on the date of his birth. Chart 25 shows Sun in 4°22' Leo and Moon at 1°01' Leo, so the Moon was near its New Moon phase at the time of his birth—actually the *Dark of the Moon* phase—since both luminaries are in the same sign.

Let's examine some of the aspects between Singleton's natal planets.

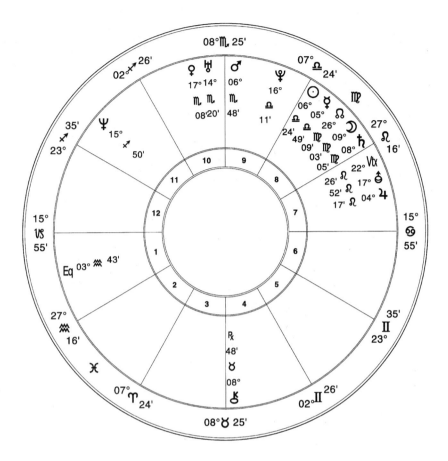

Chart 22. Event chart for time Singleton picked up Mary Bell Vincent. September 29, 1978, 3:00 P.M. PDT, Berkeley, CA 122W16, 37N52. Placidus houses. Source: Amanda Spake, "The End of the Ride—Analyzing a Sex Crime," in Mother Jones *magazine, April 1980.*

Retrograde Saturn at 1° Sagittarius trines the Sun at 4° Leo; 1° Sagittarius has been classified as a self-destructive degree, and according to astrologer Barbara Watters, Saturn in Sagittarius can indicate a lack of ethics or morals. A retrograde planet only tends to increase the negativity. Retrograde Mercury (signifying cars and travel) is conjunct Singleton's natal Pluto at 15° Cancer.

Natal Saturn closely squares Mars, denoting sex and violence. A Mars/Saturn square in a birth chart denotes destructive energy and often

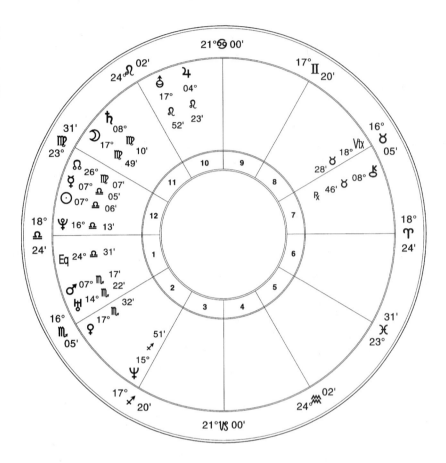

Chart 23. Event chart for time couple stopped to rescue Mary Bell Vincent. September 30, 1978, 8:00 A.M. PDT, Galt, CA, 121W18, 38N15. Placidus houses. Source: Amanda Spake, "The End of the Ride—Analyzing a Sex Crime," in Mother Jones *magazine, April 1980.*

indicates an unfortunate tendency toward cruelty. In this case, Singleton certainly proved that he lacked a conscience. In a male chart, Mars-Saturn afflictions (hard aspects) may indicate ongoing fears about sexual prowess and/or a struggle with impotence in later years. Under stressful Mars-Saturn aspects and transits, an individual may suffer depression, experience a lack of compassion, and become fascinated with thoughts of death or suicide. In her book, *Aspects of Astrology,* author Sue Tompkins associates Mars/Saturn aspects with masochism and sadism; the Marquis de Sade had natal Venus and Mars tightly squared by Saturn.

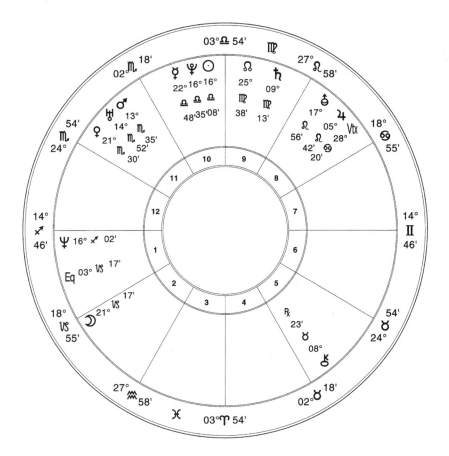

Chart 24. Event chart for Larry Singleton's arrest at his wife's home. October 9, 1978, 12:01 P.M. PDT, Sparks, NV, 119W43, 39N36. Placidus houses. Source: Amanda Spake, "The End of the Ride—Analyzing a Sex Crime," in Mother Jones magazine, April 1980.

Planetary placements at 25° Sagittarius often indicate alcoholism; Singleton's energy-draining South Node in this degree exactly trines Neptune (escapism) in the pleasure-loving sign Leo. Immediately after his arrest, Singleton could give no reason for what he'd done other than to say he'd been drinking. His neighbors seemed surprised by his arrest, as he apparently had never been in trouble before. In fact, they considered him a rather good neighbor.

The sunrise chart, when progressed to the date of the crime, September 29, 1978 (see Chart 25) shows that the natal Midheaven (reputation)

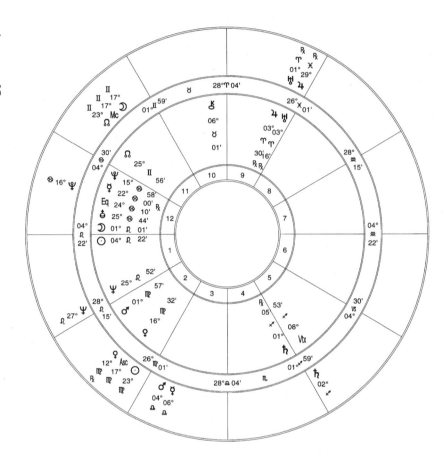

Chart 25. Singleton's sunrise birth chart, progressed to crime: September 29, 1978. July 28, 1927, 5:53:37 A.M. EST, Tampa, FL, 82W27, 27N57. Placidus houses. Source: Amanda Spake, "The End of the Ride—Analyzing a Sex Crime," in Mother Jones magazine, April 1980.

and the progressed Moon have both moved to 17° Gemini, a homicidal degree, according to Charles Carter's *Enctclopedia of Psychological Astrology*. When afflicted, 17° Gemini/Sagittarius may also indicate impotence or other sexual problems in a male chart. Singleton was fifty-one years old in 1978 and had recently separated from his second wife, although he was apparently attempting a reconciliation with her.

Singleton's progressed Midheaven (MC) degree at 17° Gemini squares natal Venus and conjoins his natal Mars/Uranus midpoint at 17°36'

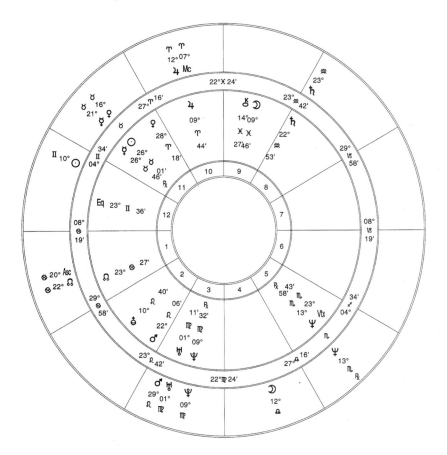

Chart 26. Natal chart for Mary Bell Vincent, progressed to the crime on September 29, 1978. Born May 17, 1963, 8:35:55 A.M. PDT (rectified from 8:31 A.M.: see below), El Centro, CA, 115W34, 32N48. Placidus houses. Source: Birth certificate obtained by Edna Rowland.

Gemini; an accident axis. Mars is inconjunct Uranus at his birth.

Singleton's progressed Ascendant at 17° Virgo squares his progressed MC, and is separating by a one degree orb from a conjunction with his natal Venus (young females) at 16° Virgo. In his natal chart, Venus is sextile Pluto and Mercury, and semisquare the Sun, which rules his physical vitality and masculine ego. Venus so heavily accented by progressions suggests that he was destined to meet a female who would change the course of his life forever. Unfortunately, this was a meeting with tragic results, particularly because the female was a minor. Singleton's solar MC is exactly conjunct Mary Bell's natal Venus at 28° Aries.

According to Mary Bell Vincent's birth certificate, she was born May 17, 1963, at 8:31 A.M. PDT in El Centro, California, the daughter of Leoncia Dabu and Herbert Clifford Vincent. I have rectified Mary Bell's time of birth to 8:35:55 A.M. PDT, or four minutes and fifty-five seconds later than the time given on her birth certificate, to conform with her prenatal epoch on July 28, 1962. Chart 26, for this rectified birth time, shows an Ascendant of 8°19' Cancer and a Midheaven of 22°24' Pisces. The Sun occupies 26° Taurus and the natal Moon is at 9°47' Pisces. This rectification of approximately five minutes moves her Midheaven and Ascendant forward about one degree. After examining her natal aspects, we'll check this rectified chart for accuracy by progressing her planets and angles to the date of the crime—September 29, 1978.

Mary Bell's birth chart shows her ruling planet, the Moon, in the watery, emotional sign of Pisces, exactly opposed to Pluto (rape and murder). Mars, a violent planet, is exactly opposed to Saturn, just one degree from the cusp of her 3rd house of travel and short trips. This is a warning to be cautious when traveling that may have saved Mary Bell had she known about it. Jupiter squares the Ascendant and is inconjunct Pluto in the fatal ninth degree of Virgo.

The synastry aspects between Singleton's and Mary Bell's charts are even more explosive. When the two met, Singleton's progressed Sun at 23°43' Virgo was conjunct Mary Bell's IC (4th house cusp) and opposing her 22°24' Pisces natal MC. His progressed Sun was also sextile her natal Vertex, trine her South Node, inconjunct her natal Saturn, and square her Equatorial Ascendant at 23° Gemini. Mary Bell's Pluto at 9° Virgo, a death planet in a homicidal degree, conjoins Singleton's Venus/Mars midpoint in Virgo and widely squares his Saturn in the sign of Sagittarius (morals and ethics), activating this part of his natal chart. According to astrologer Charles Carter, the 9th degree of the mutable signs indicates a homicidal tendency. On the day she hitched the tragic ride with him, a Moon/Saturn conjunction in 8° Virgo fell almost exactly on her natal Pluto at 9° Virgo in her 3rd house of travel and opposed her natal Moon at 9° Pisces.

Mary Bell's natal Uranus in 1° Virgo exactly conjoins Singleton's Mars at 1° Virgo, an impulsive, accident-provoking combination. Her Uranus, symbolizing the new or younger generation, also makes an exact ninety-degree aspect to his Saturn, the older generation. The square between these two planets is a violent aspect that sometimes provokes sudden, unexpected conflict or ruthless behavior. As mentioned already, the Mars/Saturn or Mars/Uranus aspect is not a happy blend, especially in synastry or comparison charts. These two planetary combinations must be handled with care and caution. Saturn puts a damper on the actions Mars wants to indulge in, resulting in frustration that eventually erupts as unwarranted cruelty, hostility, or harsh punishment. "Revenge is sweet" may be the negative motivation here. Mars/Saturn afflictions certainly encourage rather than discourage hasty, ill-considered reactions to stress. Transiting Saturn at 8° Virgo is conjunct Mary Bell's natal Pluto at the time of the crime, and square Singleton's natal Vertex at 8° Sagittarius. This Saturn/Pluto aspect can be interpreted as an older man who seeks retribution by raping. Mary Bell's progressed Sun at 10° Gemini is separating from the square to her natal Pluto and Moon, as well. These Sun/Pluto aspects occur frequently in rape cases.

On the day of the crime, transiting Saturn at 8°05' Virgo is conjunct Singleton's natal Venus/Mars midpoint at 9°14' Virgo. Ebertin, in *The Combination of Stellar Influences* describes this aspect as: "Inhibitions in love-relationship, an inclination to adultery, an abnormal or pathological sex-expression, a separation in love." 9° Virgo is repeatedly aspected in both Singleton's and Mary Bell's charts. The transiting Moon is at 9° Virgo, applying to a conjunction with Singleton's natal Venus and square his Vertex at the time he picked Mary Bell up on September 29. There is also a Moon/Saturn (female meets older man) conjunction in 8° Virgo on the day of the crime. All this activity at 8 and 9° Pisces/Virgo is activating Mary Bell's natal Moon/Pluto opposition. Transiting Neptune, a slow-moving outer planet, at 15° Sagittarius, closely squares Singleton's natal Venus in Virgo on the day of the crime; this probably represents his long-standing battle with alcohol.

See Chart 24 for the transits at the time Singleton was arrested in Sparks, Nevada, on October 9, 1978, ten days after the crime. Transiting

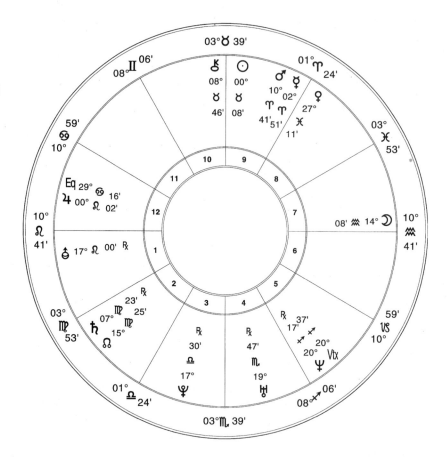

Chart 27. Event chart for Larry Singleton's sentencing to fourteen years. April 20, 1979, 12:01 P.M. PST, San Diego, CA, 117W09, 32N43. Placidus houses. Source: Amanda Spake, "The End of the Ride—Analyzing a Sex Crime," in Mother Jones *magazine, April 1980.*

Sun and Pluto are both exactly conjunct his natal Mars/Saturn midpoint at 16°31' Libra. According to *The Combination of Stellar Influences*, this Pluto-occupied midpoint implies the "intervening of a Higher Power, bodily injury, or harm." Both transiting Sun and Pluto are trine his progressed Midheaven/Moon conjunction in 17° Gemini and semisquare his natal Mars and Saturn. Sagittarius is rising and the chart ruler, Jupiter, representing justice, is conjunct his natal Leo Sun. Transiting Mars is one degree from a conjunction to transiting Uranus at 14° Scorpio, squaring his

Leo Sun and Moon. (Note: Singleton's natal Moon may be in a later degree of Leo if he was born in the afternoon or night rather than the early morning hours as his sunrise chart indicates.)

On the day Singleton was born, the Moon traveled from 28° Cancer to 11° Leo. If both luminaries were occupying Leo at his birth, this would account for his large dose of ego, perhaps making him overly conscious of his masculine image.

During the summer of 1978, Singleton's daughter had left home, and he was living alone. He had separated from his second wife, Mary Collins who said that after violent episodes following heavy drinking, he claimed not to recall the incidents. His first wife also claimed he beat her with his fists and raped her.

At his trial, Singleton readily admitted he'd been drinking grain alcohol on the day he attacked Mary Bell. This may have contributed to the lapses in his memory and explain why his story and Mary Bell Vincent's recollections didn't match. He said the girl told him she was twenty or twenty-one years old. This is only one of many ways in which their stories at the trial differed.

Eventually, Singleton realized that things weren't going as well as he'd expected, and his strategy quickly changed. He pleaded not guilty, saying he had acted in self-defense, and stuck stubbornly to his story throughout the trial and afterward. His excuse for the rape was that he "thought Mary Bell was a prostitute." Mary Bell was only fifteen; the jury didn't buy his story.

In response to the tremendous amount of pre-trial publicity, the trial was moved to San Diego, California. Singleton was found guilty of rape, sodomy, oral copulation, kidnapping, mayhem, and attempted murder. Seven months later, on April 20, 1979 (see Chart 27), he was sentenced by Judge Earl Maas, Jr. to a maximum of fourteen years and four months. He was sent to the San Diego jail, then to the Chino State Prison, and finally to San Quentin.

Unlike some Leos who welcome publicity, Singleton seldom granted interviews while in prison, but journalist Amanda Spake carried on a correspondence with the prisoner while he was in San Quentin. Spake later wrote an article about Singleton, "The End of the Ride—Analyzing a Sex

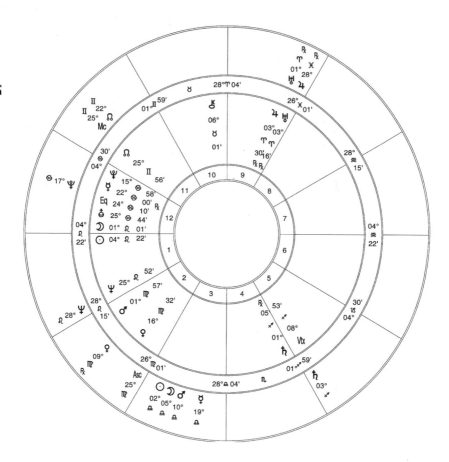

Chart 28. Singleton's sunrise birth chart (data from Chart 25) progressed to his release from prison on April 25, 1987. Source: Baton Rouge Morning Advocate newspaper, April 4, 1988.

Crime," for the April 1980 issue of *Mother Jones*. In Spake's article, she states that Singleton's view of women is "typical of males born in his generation...women are either wives or whores." Spake's analysis is based on her subjective impressions and correspondence with Singleton, and this judgement certainly fits his Venus in Virgo placement. Venus in Virgo square the Moon's Nodes denotes that his emotions and feelings toward women may have been molded by his early childhood experiences.

Venus rules Singleton's Libra 4th house (parent of opposite sex and family heritage), but since Scorpio is intercepted in that house, and Scorpio is ruled by the violent planets Mars and Pluto, all of these 4th house rulers are related. Venus makes a separating sextile aspect to Pluto. Mars is in an exact square to Saturn, the lone occupant of his 4th house. His victim, too, has an exact Mars/Saturn opposition in her natal chart, indicating much suffering and pain while traveling, since the opposition falls on the cusps of her 3rd and 9th houses. Hard Mars/Saturn aspects are often considered difficult aspects to overcome, mainly since melancholy and depression keep the individual unbalanced and tempted to overcompensate when they feel frustrated.

Note that Singleton's prenatal eclipse point (PE) at 6°31' Cancer is conjunct Mary Bell's natal Ascendant at 8° Cancer. Her prenatal eclipse point at 4°52' Aquarius exactly opposes Singleton's natal Sun at 4°22' Leo. On the day she hitched a ride with him, transiting Jupiter at 4° Leo was exactly opposite her PE (fated encounters), and transiting Mars at 6° Scorpio was square that point.

Epilogue

Singleton was one of eight children raised in strict Southern Baptist tradition. After quitting school in the eleventh grade, he went to work for the railroad, and later enlisted in the United States Coast Guard. At the time of the crime, September 29, 1978, he resided in San Pablo, separated from his second wife.

In Singleton's chart, many aspects and occupied areas signify a streak of cruelty in his nature. It's obvious that he harbored sadistic impulses or he couldn't have committed such a brutal crime. He also has Neptune at 25° Leo trine the Nodes and in an out-of-sign conjunction with his natal Mars. According to astrologer Charles Carter, the 25th degree of the fixed signs is prone to alcoholism or drug-taking when afflicted, especially when accompanied by a Mars/Neptune aspect. Alcoholism contributed greatly to Singleton's crimes.

On April 25, 1987, the sixty-year-old convict was released ahead of schedule because he had been a "model prisoner." Singleton had served nine years and eleven months of his fourteen-year, four-month sentence. See Chart 28 for progressions at Singleton's release; progressed Sun, his Sun-sign ruler, in 2° Libra, opposes natal Uranus (freedom), and the progressed

Ascendant at 25°57' Virgo squares his natal Nodes and transiting Uranus. During his first year of parole, he was forced to live temporarily in a trailer at the state prison, mainly because there was so much controversy about his early release and future residence. No matter where authorities tried to place him, infuriated residents of nearby communities attempted to ban him from living in their towns. Mary Collins, his former wife, offered him a home, but this request was refused by the parole board. To this date, Singleton's residence since his release from prison has not been revealed.

As for Mary Bell, she's a survivor if there ever was one, and has already demonstrated the great strength and endurance typical of a Taurus Sun native. According to an article in *People* magazine, Mary has succeeded in putting the past behind her. She has moved to a new location and is now married and the proud mother of several children. All who admire her courage wish that her trials and tribulations be few and that her life be full and rewarding as she grows into womanhood.

AP/ Wide World Photos

Chapter Seven

The End of an Affair

Dr. Tarnower's Last Supper

Dr. Herman Tarnower, author of the popular best-seller *The Complete Scarsdale Medical Diet*, entertained Lynne Tryforos and Debbie Raizes at a dinner in his home on March 10, 1980. His two guests left early, and the doctor went to bed at about

8:30 P.M. Little did he know what lay ahead, and that the evening's gathering had been his last supper.

Earlier, Dr. Tarnower had received an emergency phone call from his patient and mistress, Jean Harris. On March 6, she had exhausted her supply of the prescription medicine Desoxyn, usually supplied by the doctor. Suffering from severe withdrawal symptoms and the frustration of being in love with an unfaithful lover, Harris was in no mood for compromise. She insisted on coming immediately to his Westchester estate in Purchase, New York, even though Tarnower tried to persuade her to wait until the following day. She was angry because her earlier phone calls to him had been ignored. His servants often intercepted his calls and lied to Harris when she asked if the doctor was at home.

Feeling depressed and frustrated during the previous few days, Harris had made a new will and written a long letter to Dr. Tarnower in which she claimed she wanted to kill herself on his premises.

Since 1977, Harris had been the headmistress of the Madeira School for young girls in McLean, Virginia. A former teacher, she had ventured into school administration mainly for financial reasons. Her job was prestigious, but stressful. She had recently had an exceptionally bad day on the job and was thinking of resigning. One of her Madeira School colleagues had given her a bouquet of flowers, hoping to help change her mood.

After driving five hours from Virginia to New York in her blue Chrysler, Harris arrived at Tarnower's house on March 10 at about 10:40 P.M. EST. In one hand she held the flowers; in the other, her purse, concealing a .32 caliber revolver purchased a year and a half earlier. See Chart 29 for the transits on her arrival.

Shortly after 11:00 P.M. EST, Dr. Tarnower's live-in cook, Suzanne Van der Vreken, heard the doctor's bedroom buzzer. When she answered the call, she heard angry voices in the background and then a shot.

When Tarnower didn't respond, she immediately phoned the police and then woke her husband, Henri. See Chart 30 for transits at the time of the shootings. They ran upstairs to Dr. Tarnower's bedroom and were met by Jean Harris running down the stairs. Harris left the house, but returned a few minutes later with a police officer behind her. She said she had gone "to call for help at a nearby phone booth." When the officer

Chart 29: Event chart for Jean Harris' arrival at Dr. Herman Tarnower's house. March 10, 1980, 10:40 P.M. EST, Purchase, NY, 73W43, 41N02. Source: Charlotte Ann Tutor's article "Murder in Scarsdale" in American Astrology magazine, September 1988.

asked her who was responsible for the shooting, she readily admitted that she had shot the man who had been her lover for over thirteen years. She showed him the empty gun, a Harrington Richardson revolver, which she had put in her car.

Dr. Tarnower was slumped between two twin beds and covered with blood from four bullet wounds, his pulse barely perceptible. He was taken to St. Agnes Hospital in White Plains where he was pronounced dead at 11:58 P.M. EST; see Chart 31. This chart was erected for the time of

Chart 30. Event chart for Jean Harris' fatal shooting of Dr. Herman Tarnower. March 10, 1980, 11:00 P.M. EST, Purchase, NY, 73W43, 41No2. Source: Charlotte Ann Tutor's article "Murder in Scarsdale" in American Astrology magazine, September 1988, and Diana Trilling's book Mrs. Harris: The Death of the Scarsdale Diet Doctor.

death on March 10, 1980, in White Plains, New York. Note the MC at 18°51' Virgo and the Ascendant at 2°37' Sagittarius. We'll refer to this chart again later on.

Jean Harris was immediately arrested and taken to the Harrison police station. She was first charged with assault, and later with second degree murder when Dr. Tarnower died. There were also additional felony charges because her gun was licensed in Virginia, not in New York. Joel

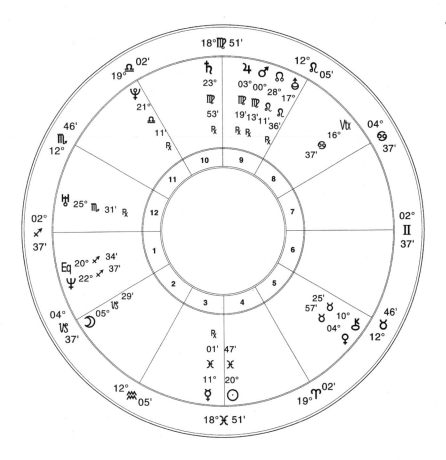

Chart 31. Event chart for the time of death of Dr. Herman Tarnower. March 10, 1980, 11:58
P.M. EST, White Plains, NY, 73W46, 41No2. Source: Charlotte Ann Tutor's article "Murder
in Scarsdale" in American Astrology magazine, September 1988, gives 11:55 P.M. EST.

Aurnou, her attorney, obtained her release on $40,000 bail the next day.

Was this a crime of passion and jealousy? It's clear that Harris had
reason to be jealous of Lynne Tryforos, Dr. Tarnower's 36-year-old office assistant at the Scarsdale Medical Center. Not only did Tryforos see
the doctor on a daily basis, but. as Harris had recently learned, they had
been having an off-and-on affair for the previous five years. Tryforos had
been spending her nights with the doctor, and she was already beginning
to replace Jean Harris in his affections, or so Harris feared. The two had

recently returned from a ten-day trip in February, and Tarnower had openly stated that he and Tryforos were planning another trip together in the very near future. When Harris arrived at his house on the night of the shooting, she found underwear and nightgowns belonging to Tryforos in Tarnower's bedroom and bathroom.

Harris and Tarnower, although very different, were nevertheless attracted to each other. To understand this murder case, we must compare their personalities.

Dr. Tarnower was the son of Eastern European Jewish immigrants; his father was Harry T. Tarnower. Dr. Tarnower was born on March 18, 1910, in Brooklyn, New York; time unknown. Since the hour of birth is not available, we'll use a derived birth time (see Chart 32), based on his death chart.

We do know the time of Dr. Tarnower's death (see Chart 31); therefore, this would be the perfect time to demonstrate the time-of-death formula for rectification as described in the preface to this book. I've experimented with this method for rectifying unknown birth times, and am happy to report that it works well when the time of death has been carefully recorded.

One of the angles of the birth chart usually rises at the time of death; this is especially true of the 4th house cusp of the birth chart. Thus, the steps of rectification are as follows:

- Place the Ascendant's degree (or angle) at the time of death on the natal 4th house cusp of the birth chart;
- After finding the corresponding MC or opposite degree, look up the proper Ascendant degree for the longitude and latitude of the birthplace;
- Place this Ascendant on the 1st house cusp of the birth chart. (Dalton's Table of Houses is a handy tool for this purpose).

Using this method, we substitute 2°37' Sagittarius, the Ascendant of the death chart, for the 4th house cusp of Dr. Tarnower's birth chart. The corresponding MC at 2°37' Gemini places 6°40' Virgo on the Ascendant at the latitude and longitude of his birthplace, Brooklyn, New York, giving us a speculative birth time of 4:15:44 P.M. EST. Before acceptance, the

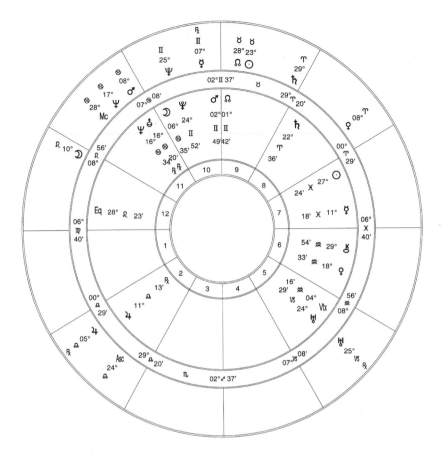

Chart 32. *Speculative birth chart for Dr. Herman Tarnower, progressed to Harris engagement, May 15, 1967. Born March 18, 1910, projected time 4:15:44 P.M. EST, Brooklyn, NY, 73W56, 40N38. Source: Shana Alexander's* Very Much a Lady *(date and place of birth only).*

chart must pass the *final* test, so we'll check it with important events in Dr. Tarnower's life.

Let's see how closely Chart 32 fits the known facts in the doctor's life: Virgo, the health sign, is rising and clearly depicts his medical profession and preferred bachelor status. Mars culminating on the Midheaven indicates the practice of surgery—heart surgery, in this case. The Moon and Pluto occupy the 10th house, and Pluto opposes the doctor's prenatal eclipse point at 20°11' Sagittarius, falling in his 4th house. The natal chart ruler, Mercury, is in 11° Pisces in the 7th house. He was tall and lanky, so an angular Mercury opposing the Ascendant describes these physical characteristics well, and portrays his literary aspirations. The Sun at 27° Pisces is the second occupant of the 7th house; it sextiles Mars and Uranus, and squares Pluto.

The elusive and sometimes deceptive planet, Neptune, rules the 7th house of marriage. Neptune, the Sun sign ruler, trines his chart ruler, Mercury, in the 7th house, and squares Saturn in the 8th house of death. Saturn rules his 5th house of courtship and love affairs; the doctor never married and had no children. He was the perennial bachelor.

In my opinion, the Virgo Ascendant fits him well. Virgo rules the intestines, and Virgo types, in addition to being attracted to the medical profession, are often hypochondriacs. Tarnower was known to take a daily laxative, mixed with applesauce.

Jean Harris' natal Moon incidentally, occupies the earth sign Virgo, and trines her Taurus Sun. Tarnower was her doctor, as well as her lover—a fact that we may sometimes forget. For the previous nine years, she had been taking prescription drugs, such as Desoxyn or methamphetamine, which he prescribed for her.

According to Michel Gauquelin, the Moon rules writers. Appropriately, it is exactly sextile the Ascendant degree in Dr. Tarnower's chart. The Moon is strong in its own sign—Cancer—which rules food. So the doctor wrote a diet cookbook that brought him much public esteem. Gemini on the MC or 10th house cusp is another significant indicator of a writer, or one who deals with words. In the natal chart, Mars, ruler of the 8th house of death, conjunct the MC, opposite the South Node, very appropriately signifies his tragic, violent death. The South Node at 1° Gemini is closely conjunct the 4th house cusp (his own death), and semisquare his Neptune-Transpluto (Bacchus) conjunction at 16° Cancer. Close and appropriate progressions to this Virgo Ascendant birth chart on the date of his death confirm and verify its amazing accuracy! But for now, let's examine a few more biographical facts about Dr. Tarnower's life.

There's no doubt that this reputable cardiologist was an ambitious social climber. He was proud of his membership in the German Jewish Country Club, and built his home in an exclusive neighborhood in the

Chart 33. Sunrise chart for Jean Harris, progressed to Tarnower engagement, May 15, 1967. Born April 27, 1923. Sunrise chart calculated for 4:58:20 A.M. CST, Chicago, IL, 87W39, 41N52. Source: Birth date and place confirmed by Harris to author; she could not provide time.

wealthy suburb of Purchase, New York. In 1978, he wrote his best-selling diet book. At the time of his death, the book was in its tenth printing.

Jean Struven (Jean Harris) was born on April 27, 1923, to Mr. and Mrs. Albert Struven, an Episcopalian family from Chicago, Illinois; her birth time is unknown. This Chicago birth data appears in Diana Trilling's book, *Mrs. Harris*, and I have confirmed it with Jean Harris. Because the time of birth is unknown, we'll use a sunrise chart; see Chart 33. On the day of birth, sunrise occurred at 4:58:20 A.M. CST in Chicago,

Illinois. Although not as revealing as a natal chart, it's adequate for comparison purposes and can be progressed.

When she met Dr. Tarnower, Harris was supporting two young sons, David and James, from a nineteen-year-marriage to James Harris, which ended in divorce in 1965. When her ex-husband died, Harris raised her sons alone. Tarnower and Harris met at a dinner party on December 6, 1966, and they were immediately attracted to each other. They took a number of expensive trips around the world together, and on May 15, 1967, Tarnower proposed marriage, giving Harris a huge diamond engagement ring said to be worth $35,000. A few months later, he retracted his marriage proposal, saying that he "couldn't go through with it." He offered no further explanation, and Harris returned the ring.

During the period of the engagement, there were several contradictory progressed aspects to Tarnower's natal planets; see Chart 32. His progressed MC at 28° Cancer was making a favorable, but separating, trine to the Sun in his 7th house of marriage. At the same time, his progressed Ascendant at 24° Libra was exactly trine Pluto, but making a disruptive square aspect to Uranus, dispositor of his natal Venus at 18° Aquarius. Uranus occupies his 5th house of courtship and love affairs at birth, so the good doctor wasn't about to give up his freedom so easily. Tarnower broke the engagement, but instead of splitting up, the couple began a love affair that lasted more than thirteen years—until progressed Venus and Mercury in Harris' chart reached an explosive, unfriendly conjunction with Mars; see Chart 33. At Dr. Tarnower's request, it was an open affair that allowed both parties a certain amount of freedom (Uranus). However, over the years, it turned into a love/hate relationship that ended with the doctor's tragic death.

How do these two charts compare as far as synastry goes? Jean Harris has a Taurus Sun; she has four planets in fixed signs, so this may account for her stubborn determination to continue her affair with Tarnower, in spite of insurmountable obstacles and frustrations. Her job as headmistress of a girl's college required her to live on campus. As a result, she could no longer see Tarnower as frequently as she had before she accepted the headmistress position. Whenever she visited Tarnower,. she had to drive an exhausting five-hour trip from Virginia to Purchase, New York.

Astrologically, the main attraction between Tarnower and Harris seems to be indicated by her Venus at 1° Aries in an out-of-sign conjunction with his Sun at 27° Pisces, within his 7th house. Venus is a social planet, so this is a friendly, affectionate contact that indicates two people who share many intellectual interests as well as social contacts. Her Sun at 6° Taurus closely trines his 6° Virgo Ascendant. Although her time of birth is unknown, her natal Moon is definitely in Virgo, possibly within the allowed orb for a conjunction aspect to his natal Ascendant. This type of Moon/Ascendant contact is often seen when comparing mutual aspects between lovers. In addition, her prenatal eclipse point (PE) at 25°55' Pisces is conjunct his Sun—a karmic bond between two people.

Unfortunately, his natal Mars squares her Moon, spoiling the promised harmony. His chart ruler, Mercury, opposes her Moon, so he'd be inclined to lie to her frequently in a misguided attempt to restore harmony to their relationship. They both have Mars in the intellectual Air sign Gemini, but unfortunately this serves only to reinforce her natal Mars square Moon aspect. This is a double whammy because his Mars also squares her Moon, and squares his ruler, Mercury. A Moon/Mars square depicts a bad temper with the possibility of quarrels erupting into violence if not strictly under control. These are explosive Mars aspects. At his death, Tarnower's progressed Moon at 16° Capricorn opposes Harris' progressed Mars.

The doctor's ruling planet, Mercury, squares Mars in Gemini, so he'd be inclined to indulge briefly in verbal abuse or enjoy a battle of wits when angered. Violent Mars is angular and squares his natal Ascendant, so he could be pushed too far. On the other hand, her natal Mars square Uranus in a wide nine-degree orb, is a disruptive aspect often found in charts of those who are accident-prone or suicidal. When afflicted, this aspect denotes an individual inclined to impulsive acts, showing a notable lack of good judgment and common sense. Frequently, it indicates violent acts or accidents during which the person seems to throw caution to the winds.

Dr. Tarnower's Jupiter conjoins Harris' Saturn, which is exalted in Libra. This Jupiter/Saturn contact is traditionally regarded as an excellent business partnership aspect. According to Harris, she helped Tarnower write his best-selling diet book and was paid four thousand dollars for her contribution. Maybe this indicates they would have been more successful as business partners than as lovers.

Was this a masochistic relationship? Maybe they both had trouble defining the nature of their relationship. It seemed to be an unstructured union without any definite boundaries. Virgos are known, however, to frequently indulge in self-pity and sometimes even enjoy martyrdom. How could these tragic events happen? Why did an intelligent, well-educated woman like Jean Harris allow Tarnower to continue to be her private physician, considering the inconvenience this must have caused her? Surely she could have afforded the services of another reputable physician in her area who could have diagnosed her condition, and her drug dependence, more objectively.

Was she unconsciously attempting to weave a spider's web which would make the doctor more dependent on her? If so, the plan certainly backfired and became part of their tragic destiny. At her trial, Harris claimed the doctor's death was accidental, occurring after a struggle for the loaded gun. This contention became part of her defense. Harris insists she went to Dr. Tarnower's house planning to kill herself, rather than to kill him. Her defense lawyer failed to establish lack of premeditation. Because more than one shot was fired, it was difficult to prove that the shots were accidental.

In his will, Tarnower was exceptionally generous with his servants—another Virgo trait. Mars in his chart rules legacies, and the sixty-nine-year-old physician left Suzanne and Henri Van der Vrekens $2,000 for every year in his employ, adding up to $32,000 each. He also left Lynne Tryforos $220,000 and Jean Harris $200,000; but his married sister (Mars in Gemini) was his chief beneficiary.

Now we'll examine the outstanding transits and progressions for Dr. Tarnower's death on the night of March 10, 1980, just eight days before his seventieth birthday. Chart 31, for the time of death, shows transiting Saturn opposing Tarnower's Pisces Sun and transiting Neptune square his Sun. The planetary trio of Mars, Jupiter, and Saturn occupy Virgo, aspecting his Ascendant. The transits show a mutable T-square pattern between Saturn, Neptune, and the Sun, with the open end of the T-square in Gemini, directly opposite his natal Pluto at 24° Gemini. Neptune is

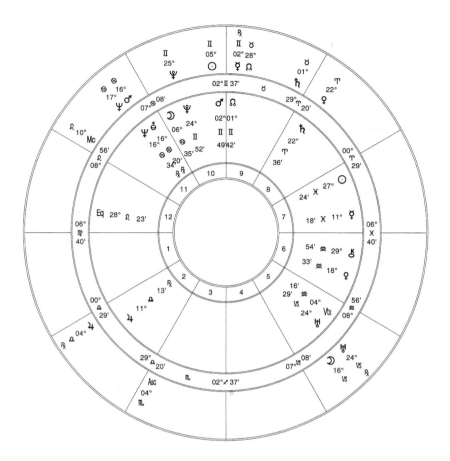

Chart 34. Tarnower's speculative birth chart progressed to his death on March 10, 1980. (See birth data: Chart 32.) Source: Shana Alexander's Very Much a Lady *for the date and time of Tarnower's death.*

conjunct his prenatal eclipse point at 20°11′ Sagittarius in his 4th house of endings, and the transiting Sun is square that point.

Chart 34, illustrating Tarnower's secondary progressions on March 10, 1980, shows his progressed Ascendant at 4° Scorpio opposing transiting Venus at 4° Taurus (indicating the presence of his Taurus mistress, Jean Harris). The progressed MC at 10° Leo is semisquare his natal Sun and sextile radical Jupiter, his 4th house ruler, while his progressed Ascendant at 4° Scorpio directly squares his natal Vertex. The progressed Sun at 5° Gemini squares his natal Virgo Ascendant; progressed Venus at 22° Aries

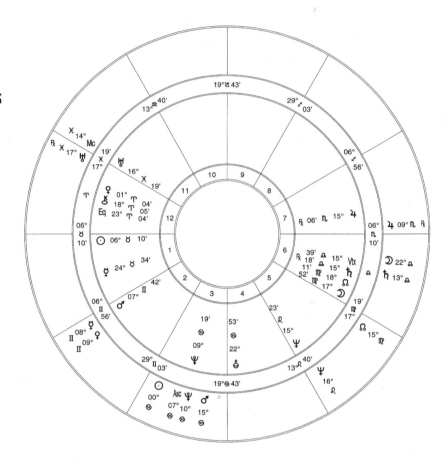

Chart 35. Harris' sunrise chart, progressed to Tarnower's murder on March 10, 1980. Born April 27, 1923. Birth chart calculated for 4:58:20 A.M. CST, Chicago, IL, 87W39, 41N52. Source: Date and place confirmed by Jean Harris to author through correspondence; actual time of birth unknown.

conjoins natal Saturn in his 8th house of death.

The aspects of the progressed Moon at Tarnower's death pinpoint the events even more accurately. His progressed Moon at 16° Capricorn is exactly opposite his natal Neptune/Transpluto conjunction at 16° Cancer, denoting his jealous, suicidal mistress. To top it all, progressed Mars, his 8th house ruler at 16° Cancer, conjoins this natal Neptune/Transpluto conjunction and exactly opposes the progressed Moon! These aspects certainly support the case for the Virgo Ascendant birth chart.

A quick look at the major progressions in Jean Harris' chart (see Chart 35) for the death of Dr. Tarnower shows the following aspects: Progressed Sun at 0°50' Cancer exactly square her natal Venus; progressed Venus (her Sun sign ruler) conjunct progressed Mercury and semisextile Pluto. Her progressed Ascendant at 7° Cancer conjoins Tarnower's natal Moon at 6° Cancer. These aspects indicate that she continued to have strong feelings for the doctor, despite their differences and growing estrangement. Her desperation was sharpened by the fact that her health was failing rapidly, as shown by the following aspects to her natal planets; the progressed South Node (a stressful energy drain in Pisces) is conjunct natal Uranus and her progressed MC, showing restricted freedom. Progressed Mars at 15° Cancer is square natal Saturn. The applying square between Mars and Saturn indicates her rapidly increasing stress, anger, and depression. The progressed MC at 14° Pisces trines progressed Mars and natal Jupiter and forms a Yod configuration aspect to her natal Neptune and Saturn. Her progressed Mars at 15° Cancer is conjunct Tarnower's progressed Mars at 16° Cancer.

Almost a year later, on February 24, 1981, the jury found Jean Harris guilty of murder in the second degree. One month later, on March 20, Judge Leggett sentenced Harris to prison for fifteen years to life. She was taken to Bedford Hills Correctional Facility, New York State's maximum security prison for women.

Epilogue

While in prison, Jean Harris became an advocate for women prisoners and their children, and worked with a nun at the Children's Center of the Bedford Hills Correctional Facility. Together, they have created a place for mothers and children to play and visit together. Harris has used her considerable teaching skills to start parenting courses and birth programs for pregnant prisoners.

With Chiron (the Healer) in her 12th house ruling jails and institutions, and her progressed Moon opposite Chiron at the time of her sentencing on March 20, 1981, Harris was likely to find prison a therapeutic experience. By helping needy women in prison, she created a positive use for her Pisces planets and Nodes.

I believe Harris may have a Capricorn Ascendant, but this is only a guess. She definitely has executive skills, and Capricorn rising would probably put her ruler, Saturn, in Libra in the 10th house of professional skills. Saturn in the 10th is often called "the dreaded Napoleon aspect" since it sometimes signals a sudden fall from grace and usually signifies a person too proud for their own good. Humility is the lesson this individual must learn before finding happiness. With the Moon in Virgo conjunct her North Node, service to others is a necessity for Harris, not just an option.

In her autobiography, *Stranger in Two Worlds*, Harris describes prison conditions and tells her own story. The book was published in 1986 by Macmillan Publishing Co. Under New York law, she cannot earn any profits from the book. Although Governor Mario Cuomo had refused three times before, he finally granted her clemency after she had served twelve years in prison. Harris had undergone coronary bypass surgery and this, along with the fact that she was a model prisoner, evidently softened his heart.

Part II:

The Link Between Suicide & Homicide

Chapter Eight

Suicide

The Last Choice

Suicide is found in all societies, at all ages, in all social groups, and among both sexes. Each year there are about 25,000 to 30,000 suicides recorded in the United States. This figure could actually be as high as 60,000, because many suicides are recorded as accidents. It is America's eleventh leading cause of death.

Researchers have found that suicide statistics show a seasonal pattern in the northern hemisphere. Suicide rates reach a peak in April and May, and taper off in December and January. Blachly's and Fairly's statistics for a twenty-four-hour cycle reveal more suicides occur between noon and 6:00 P.M. than between midnight and 6:00 A.M. Sunday is the day most often chosen by women, while men prefer Monday.

Hardly anyone who commits suicide actually wants to die. Although this may seem to be a contradictory statement, it reflects the ambivalent, confused state of mind that precedes most suicide attempts. Its truth can be backed by irrefutable facts. Among victims, the expectation that suicide will solve some insurmountable problem is usually very high. Depression sometimes leads to a state of general confusion in which all problems are lumped together so that the person no longer has a clear idea of just what troubles them the most. Despondency often leads to hopelessness; then comes the decision to end it all. Contrary to common beliefs, suicide rarely occurs at the lowest moment of depression; it is more apt to occur just as depression has begun to diminish. Only then, it seems, does a person have enough energy to commit the act—to make the last choice.

According to current statistics (as of this writing) the rate for teenage suicide is increasing rapidly. Women attempt suicide more frequently than men. However, actual rates for completed or successful suicides are much higher for men than for women This is partly because men tend to choose more lethal methods, leaving less time for intervention or rescue attempts. Men also have more experience with a wider variety of weapons, especially if they have been in the military. In the next few pages, we'll explore why men and women differ so greatly in their choice of weapons and their suicidal behavior.

Over the past few years, many suicide prevention centers have sprung up all over the United States. The belief that a person must be crazy to take his or her own life is slowly dissolving in the light of new facts gathered by these centers and follow-up studies made by qualified researchers. It's been observed that a certain state of mind characterizes most suicide attempts and may even be a prerequisite for the act itself.

Astrologers could contribute greatly to these areas of research. According to astrologer and mythologist Demitra George in her book *Mysteries of the Dark Moon*, "More suicides occur in the thirty days preceding a birthday than all the rest of the year." Ethics about predicting death need not interfere here because astrology can be employed as a preventive measure. By examining and studying the birth charts of those who have made attempts to kill themselves, astrologers may be able to spot the potential suicide before it is too late. Astrology, when combined with other professional and common-sense methods of suicide prevention, might go a long way toward helping remove this major killer.

Competent psychological astrologers and counsellors are trained to observe and interpret troublesome patterns of behavior and personality traits in an individual's birth chart. For example, a susceptibility to confused, unrealistic hopes and expectations may be interpreted from Neptune afflictions to Mercury (mentality) or to the luminaries, since the Sun and Moon show basic characteristics. Likewise, susceptibility to self-pity or melancholy may be surmised from numerous afflictions between the luminaries and Saturn, or by unfavorable aspects between Saturn and the Ascendant, or its rulers. Natal Mercury/Saturn or Jupiter/Saturn oppositions often indicate a temperament subject to extreme moods of elation and manic depression, causing a see-saw effect that lifts the individual up one day and drops him or her down the next for no apparent reason.

The term *afflictions*, as used here, means hard aspects such as squares, semisquares, oppositions, or conjunctions with malefic planets like Mars, Saturn, Uranus, and Neptune. These latter planets are frequently prominent and heavily afflicted in suicide charts. Thus, a conjunction of Neptune and the Moon would be considered an affliction because the malefic influence of Neptune is greatly intensified. Neptune afflictions generally seem to cloud the issues, making it difficult to distinguish clearly between truth and falsehood. Mars afflictions indicate aggressive, violent tendencies. Aspects from Uranus may indicate the danger of uncontrolled, impulsive actions.

According to suicide research by the Church of Light, the *timing* of a suicidal act usually coincides with a progressed aspect to the ruler of the 12th house. As we know, the 12th house rules secrets, loneliness, skeletons in the closet, and private enemies. It also is related to hospitals and other types of institutions where a person who has attempted suicide sometimes ends up. Successful suicides must be arranged for a time when the person will have enough privacy to ensure they won't be interrupted or prevented from completing the act. Since suicide generally requires some degree of privacy and secrecy, this may account for the astrological emphasis on the 12th house.

Diagnosing mental illness of any kind is usually outside the province of the astrologer, and mental disturbance may or may not be present during a suicide attempt, but neurotic tendencies may be reflected in the natal chart by heavy afflictions to the rulers of the 3rd and 12th houses, or planets therein. Stressful aspects by progressed or transiting planets may aggravate or accent these trouble spots if they exist. If the 12th house contains several planets that receive heavy afflictions, there may be a tendency toward extreme introversion, loneliness, or isolation from the world. These abnormal or neurotic tendencies may manifest either constructively or destructively, depending on other factors in the chart, but if erratic behavior is consistently observed, the astrologer should refer the client to a clinical psychologist or licensed psychiatrist.

Manly P. Hall and Charles Carter, well-known research astrologers, have done valuable statistical work uncovering the significant *sign and house positions* of natal planets in the charts of people who have committed suicide. Hall and Carter found that people with planets in Cardinal and Mutable signs were more prone to accidents than those with planets in Fixed signs, with the exception of Leo, especially if it is rising. Despite differences in their individual findings, both astrologers chose Leo as the most probable rising sign in the charts of people who are accident- and/or suicide-prone. Libra and Pisces were the next most frequent Ascendant signs, and the late British astrologer Charles Carter discovered that Sagittarius is frequently found on the Ascendant in charts of drowning victims.

The psychological reason for the high statistical percentage of Leo Ascendants in suicide cases may be that Leo is a proud, inflexible, Fixed sign. Although Leo is one of the most courageous and generous signs, Leo people may be less generous to themselves than they are to others. They may be less willing than other signs to change their goals in life, regardless of

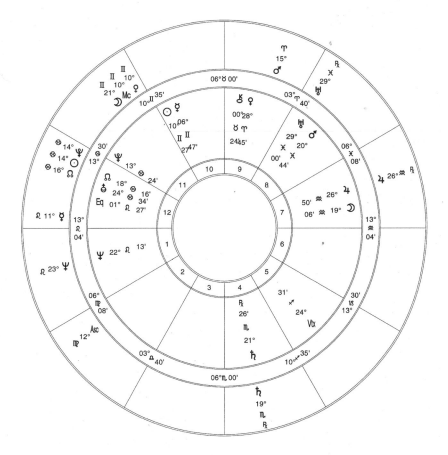

Chart 36. Marilyn Monroe. Birth chart progressed to her death on August 4, 1962. Born June 1, 1926, 9:30 A.M. PST, Los Angeles, CA 118W15, 34N03. Sources: Robert Slatzer, The Curious Death of Marilyn Monroe, (a photograph of Marilyn's birth certificate appears in the back of the book) and Lois Rodden, Profiles of Women, pg. 81; both sources concur.

their limitations. When they fail, they don't always snap back as quickly as others, despite their jovial nature. Leo types are apt to brag about their successes and dramatize personal victories to such an extent that they can't tolerate the thought of losing face with associates. Parental love for their children usually sustains them, however and is a saving grace.

To my knowledge, there has been no previous attempt by astrologers to clearly differentiate between male and female suicides, although men and

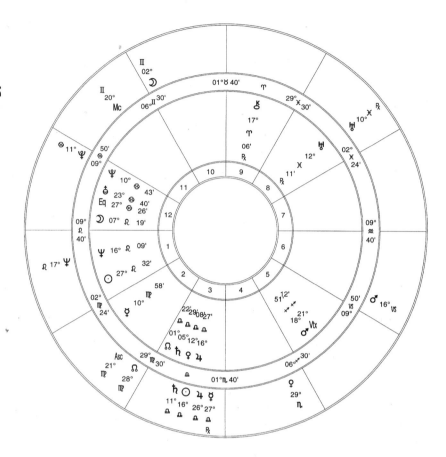

Chart 37. "Steve," a male murder-suicide. Birth chart progressed to murder on June 17, 1972. Born August 21, 1922, 3:45 A.M. CST, 85W41, 34N09. Placidus houses. Name and birthplace withheld for confidentiality, time from birth certificate. Source: Author's files.

women generally choose entirely different methods of killing themselves. In order to define and outline these basic differences, I've chosen to examine the natal birth charts of one female and one male suicide victim. Since both charts have Leo Ascendants; they will have similar house rulerships.

According to her birth certificate, the female, Norma Jean (known by most as Marilyn Monroe), was born June 1, 1926, at 9:30 A.M. PST in Los Angeles, California; see Chart 36. The Midheaven of her natal chart is at 6° Taurus; the Ascendant at 13° Leo. She died somewhere between 8:00

P.M. and midnight on Saturday, August 4, 1962, supposedly from an over-dose of sleeping pills at her home in Brentwood, California. Her death cer-tificate records her death as "a probable suicide."

The male, "Steve" (not his real name), was born August 21, 1922 at 3:45 A.M. CST. He has both his Sun and Ascendant in the fiery sign of Leo; see Chart 37. His natal Midheaven is at 2° Taurus and his Ascendant at 9° Leo. After he shot and killed his estranged wife, who was born July 27, 1930, he immediately shot himself in the head. Murder and suicide are often related, especially when a criminal wishes to avoid being caught and convicted. This murder/suicide occurred on June 17, 1972, at 7:55 A.M. CDT, when his progressed MC opposed his natal Mars (guns, shooting). Steve died at the hospital at about 9:00 A.M. CDT of the same day; his wife died at 10:12 A.M.

There are many similarities between these two birth charts besides Leo Ascendants. For instance, both have Neptune in the 1st house, Uranus in the 8th house of death (short life, speedy death), and Pluto on the 12th house cusp. In Marilyn's chart, there's a square aspect from progressed Saturn to the Moon, ruler of her 12th house, which became effective on the date of death. Progressed Mars, her 4th house ruler, squares her pro-gressed Sun-Pluto conjunction exactly on the cusp of her 12th house of secret enemies. Progressed Moon at 21° Gemini squares natal Mars in the 8th and is inconjunct natal Saturn in her 4th house of endings.

Observing the progressed aspects to the 12th house and its rulers in both of the above charts serves to confirm the previously given rule for *timing* a suicidal act.

According to Rex Bills in *The Rulership Book*, Uranus and Pluto aspects tend to show up often in suicide charts, and the 8th and 12th houses also need to be examined for occupants. The male murder-suicide chart (Chart 37) shows Steve's progressed Uranus in the 8th house making a trine as-pect to natal Pluto near the cusp of his 12th house on the date of death; the progressed Ascendant at 21° Virgo is applying to a semisquare aspect with the natal Moon, which occupies Steve's 12th house.

As we shall now show, Monroe's chart doesn't quite fit the time-of-death formula described previously for suicides: the natal Ascendant sign and degree usually rises or remains the same in a suicidal death event chart, indicating death was self-inflicted. Instead, Monroe's estimated death chart for around 11:46 P.M. PDT shows her natal Taurus MC degree rising, instead of her Leo Ascendant. We can only conclude that there is room for doubt as to whether or not she actually committed suicide. By contrast, Chart 37 does fit the time-of-death formula for suicide, since at the time of Steve's death, 5° Leo was rising on the cusp of the 1st house, or Ascendant, and this is within a four degree orb of his 9° Leo birth Ascendant. Since locations for the death and birth charts differ, this could account for the difference of four degrees.

Both charts have strongly aspected, angular Neptunes. People with high ideals nearly always have a prominent Neptune; but those with an afflicted Neptune may find it hard to adjust to unstable personal relationships, the sudden loss of a partner, marital infidelity, or deception on the part of a loved one. Marilyn Monroe was married three times during her thirty-six years, and this is shown by her Aquarius Moon in the 7th house opposite Neptune. She had a very unhappy, deprived childhood, as indicated by Saturn in the 4th house square the Moon. It is reported that, as a child, Marilyn lived for a time in an orphanage and then with several different foster parents. Her mother, represented in Marilyn's chart by her afflicted Moon square Saturn and opposite Neptune, was frequently absent and unable to function due to a series of bouts with mental illness. Marilyn saw her mother infrequently, and these visits were often traumatic.

Steve's birth chart (Chart 37) shows a violent Mars/Uranus square affecting the 5th and 8th houses. Uranus rules his 7th house of marriage; he divorced his first wife and remarried. Although Mars, co-ruler of the 4th, trines Neptune, this violent planet squares natal Mercury and Uranus, thereby forming an explosive Mutable T-square, which was triggered by transiting Saturn at 12° Gemini on the date of his death by suicide. Although athletic and interested in physical body-building sports (Mars in the 5th house), he was extremely accident-prone, had a quick temper, and liked to gamble. As shown by both the Moon and Sun conjunct Neptune and his natal Mars trine Neptune, he was much too fond of alcoholic beverages. His birth occurred during the Balsamic Dark Moon phase, when the moon was 0-45 degrees behind the Sun.

Planetary afflictions to the luminaries tend to manifest differently in male and female charts; thus, interpretation of similar aspects will be more meaningful if these sexual and psychological differences are kept in mind.

For example, in a *male* chart, the Sun symbolizes his masculine ego, whereas the Moon represents his reaction to the opposite sex. In a *female* chart, the Moon's effect is more direct because it represents her own personal feminine attributes, whereas the Sun represents important males in her life, like her father or spouse.

Men with natal Sun/Neptune afflictions (as shown in Steve's chart), frequently expect the women in their lives to live up to an impossible image or ideal. When disappointed, these men may assume the role of the disillusioned husband or lover. Both men and women with badly afflicted Neptunes at birth may be tempted to escape from their troubles into a world of fantasy, the natural domain of Neptune, through the abuse of drugs or alcohol. Their subsequent withdrawal from the world makes them increasingly hard to reach, and counseling would have to be very reality-oriented to effect the desired response.

For both men and women, the loss of love and the failure of personal relationships, as represented by afflictions of Saturn and Neptune to Venus, or unfavorable aspects from the 5th and 7th houses, may generate anxiety about the outcome of future relationships. Since the Moon-ruled female of the species often invests so much of her ego in personal relationships, loss of love may seriously endanger a woman's self-esteem. A Neptune affliction to the Moon in a female chart might make it difficult for her to be entirely realistic because of a tendency toward wishful thinking (as in Marilyn Monroe's chart). Ironically, this same Moon/Neptune opposition within angular houses made Marilyn a natural-born Hollywood star. Strong Neptune aspects often lead to career choices of acting or photography. Dreamy Neptune types may prefer glamorous lives over harsh reality.

Soft aspects such as trines and sextiles between Neptune (expectations) and Saturn (necessity) would enable a person to cope with disappointments when they arise. Hard aspects between Saturn and Neptune, as illustrated in Monroe's chart, would have just the opposite effect. They can make it difficult for people to adjust to reality, since they refuse to give up their fantasies and delusions of grandeur or persecution, no matter how far-fetched or hopeless their ideas may actually be.

In both sexes, failure of personal relationships may have disastrous results; but for women, loss of a loved one ranks as the *first* cause for suicide. When rendering a judgment on suicide potential, therefore, astrologers who do counseling would do well to judge planetary afflictions to the 3rd (siblings), 5th (romance and children), and 7th (partnerships) houses as being of greater importance in female charts, simply because these three houses deal primarily with our relationships with other people.

According to statisticians Ellis and Allen, "For our total population of white men, suicide ranks as the 8th leading cause of death, and among women as 16th." The tendency toward suicide is lower among married people, higher among those who are divorced. Twice as many single men kill themselves as married men. Wealth, or lack of it, seems insignificant; but it is more likely for a man in the white-collar professions to commit suicide than his blue-collar counterparts. Among men, loss of job (10th house), income (2nd house), or physical disability (6th house), may threaten loss of status and is most often an important contributing cause for suicide.

Because we tend to associate the ego's self-assertive qualities more readily with males than females, and Neptune is a feminine planet, Neptune afflictions to the luminaries can probably be observed more easily by examining male charts. This is because Neptune's ego-denying tendencies run counter to society's expectations of male agressiveness. Afflictions to the Sun generally manifest objectively or outwardly in actions and behavior, while Moon afflictions tend to be more subjective and not as apparent on the surface.

Men and women statistically show different preferences for their methods of death. As a rule, male suicides prefer methods that are sudden and violent, and are likely to kill themselves away from home: Conversely, females tend to choose passive and non-disfiguring methods, most often committing suicide in or near their homes. (A notable exception is Japan, a Libra country, where more males prefer a non-violent end.)

Astrological formulae describing three of the most preferred methods for *female suicides* are as follows:

1. Barbiturates or Poison. Mars/Neptune or Mars afflictions. Moon/Sun afflictions, especially when connected by aspects to planets in Virgo or Scorpio. 24 through 28 degrees of the Fixed signs. 12° Virgo and/or Pisces. 11° Cardinal signs (especially for poison, if Jupiter is in Aquarius). See Marilyn Monroe's chart for natal Pluto in a Cardinal sign, Jupiter in Aquarius, and Mars inconjunct Neptune.

2. Gas Fumes (asphyxiation). Afflictions to Saturn, especially from Mercury and Pluto. 13° of the mutable signs. Any progressed aspect from Neptune. (For an example of asphyxiation, see Chapter 11, Sylvia Plath.)

3. Drowning. Sun/Moon afflictions indicate danger near water. Moon/Neptune afflictions. Hard aspects of Neptune to a 4th house planet or its ruler. Saturn badly afflicted, usually by Neptune. Any aspect between Mercury and Saturn. Sagittarius Ascendant. The last degrees of Gemini/Sagittarius and/or Aries/Libra. The first degrees of Cancer/Capricorn and Taurus/Scorpio (especially if Mars is near 0° Taurus/Scorpio). A progressed Mars aspect. (For example, Virginia Woolf, see below.)

The British novelist, Virginia Woolf, is an example of a female drowning victim. She was born on January 25, 1882, at 12:05 P.M. GMT, in London, England, and committed suicide on March 28, 1941, by drowning herself in a river. Natal aspects were Saturn conjunct Neptune; Mercury, her ruler, square Saturn, Neptune, and Jupiter in Taurus; Moon in 0° Taurus closely conjunct Saturn and square her Aquarius Sun sign.

According to statistics, three of the most preferred *male suicide* methods are:

1. Shooting or stabbing, a Mars-ruled activity. Sun/Mars afflictions. Venus/Uranus afflictions. 17 through 23° of the Cardinal signs. 21 and 29° Aries/Libra. 1 through 5° of the other Mutable signs. 13° of all the Mutable signs. 16° of Gemini/Sagittarius. 6° of the Cardinal signs (for bullet wounds). (See Steve's chart in this chapter. He has natal Venus inconjunct Uranus, Mars in 18° Sagittarius square Uranus, and his progressed Sun was exactly square progressed Mars when he killed himself.)

2. Hanging (strangulation). All of Taurus, because it rules the throat, but especially 16° and 25° Taurus and squares to these degrees. The malefic

Fixed star, Algol, occupies 25° Taurus and indicates injuries to the neck, fractures, or violent death.

3. Jumping (out of windows or from bridges). Sun or Moon afflicted by Saturn, indicating broken bones or crushing. 15 through 19° Libra (especially 18 and 19°). Saturn in Cancer. Afflictions between planets in Cancer and Libra. 14 through 17° of all Mutable signs. Most likely Ascendants are Leo or Virgo. (Charles Stuart, who murdered his wife and unborn child on October 23, 1989, was born on December 18, 1959, at 5:16 A.M. EST in Boston, Massachusetts. This is "AA" data from the birth certificate according to Lois Rodden's *Astro Data V*. He jumped off a Boston bridge and drowned on January 4, 1990 at 6:45 A.M. EST. See the aspects for drowning.)

AP/ Wide World Photos

Chapter Nine

Was Marilyn Monroe's Death Suicide or Murder?

Almost three decades after Marilyn Monroe's alleged suicide, her strange death remains shrouded in mystery. Every book and biography written about her only seems to compound the mystery, adding one more fact and another doubt. Can astrology shed any light on the questionable circumstances surrounding her death? Did she commit suicide, or was she murdered, as Milo Speriglio asserts in his book, *The Marilyn Conspiracy?*

On Sunday, August 5, 1962, the police were notified of the death of a thirty-six-year-old woman at about 4:35 A.M. PST. Sergeant Jack Clemmons at the West Los Angeles police station was on duty to take the call. He immediately rushed to Marilyn's home where he found Dr. Ralph R. Greenson, Marilyn's psychiatrist, and Dr. Hyman Engelberg, an internist, in the bedroom. Dr. Engelberg had made the call to the police after examining Marilyn and declaring her dead. She was discovered laying face down and naked on her small bed, clutching the telephone. Dr. Greenson stated, "Marilyn Monroe died of an accidental overdose of barbiturates." Why did the two doctors wait four hours or more to call the police?

The housekeeper, Mrs. Eunice Murray, who had worked for Marilyn since November of 1961, was busy doing the laundry and other household chores when Sergeant Clemmons arrived. Mrs. Murray was not a live-in maid, but occasionally stayed overnight when needed. Marilyn's psychiatrist, Dr. Ralph R. Greenson, had asked her to stay with Marilyn the night of Saturday, August 4th. When questioned, she told Clemmons she had found Marilyn dead in her bed around midnight. She had knocked on Marilyn's locked door, and when she got no reponse, phoned Dr. Greenson immediately, who broke a window in order to enter Marilyn's bedroom. Mrs. Murray said that after Marilyn had retired to her room at about 8:00 P.M. PDT the night before, she had made and received several telephone calls. At 7:30 P.M., she received a call from Joe DiMaggio. Afterward, the housekeeper recalled that Marilyn had phoned Dr. Greenson. Strangely, the records of her phone calls on that night have disappeared.

Marilyn didn't leave a suicide note. Sergeant Clemmons noticed an empty bottle of Nembutal on her nightstand, but there was no glass of water. Nembutal capsules are powerful barbiturates taken to induce sleep. The police officer examined the adjoining bathroom and found it was being remodeled, so no water could be had from the bathroom faucets. Mrs. Murray couldn't recall having brought Marilyn any water to take her pills. Sergeant Clemmons found her rather defensive and reluctant to answer questions, preferring to let the doctors speak for her.

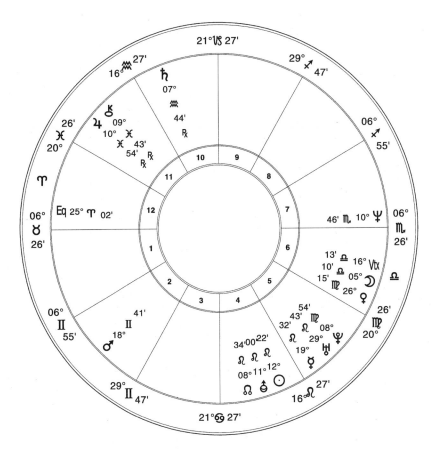

Chart 38. *Rectified estimated event chart for Marilyn Monroe's death, August 4, 1962, 11:46:11 P.M. PDT, Brentwood, CA 121W42, 37N56.* Source: The Marilyn Conspiracy *by Milo Speriglio for the date and time of her death as given by the coroner and police; see pages 12-13.*

The officer observed that Marilyn's body was in an advanced state of rigor mortis, indicating she must had been dead at least four to six hours, perhaps even six to eight hours. If we assume Sergeant Clemmons arrived at Marilyn's home at about 5 A.M. PDT, she must have died some time between 9 P.M. and midnight PDT the previous day.

According to our astrological calculations, we estimate that the most likely time of death was 11:46:11 P.M. PDT on August 4, when her 6°27' Scorpio natal 4th house cusp occupied the 7th house angle of death (see Chart 38). Before we demonstrate how we arrived at this estimated time of death by the time-of-death formula, let's first take a look at Marilyn's birth chart and attempt to rectify it or confirm the given time of birth.

Lois Rodden's *Profiles of Women* lists Marilyn's birth time, from her birth certificate, as 9:30 A.M. PST. Norma Jean Mortenson was born to Gladys Monroe Baker on June 1, 1926, in a Los Angeles, California hospital; father unknown. A photocopy of this birth certificate is included in the back of one of Marilyn's biographies, *The Curious Life and Death of Marilyn Monroe*, by Robert F. Slatzer. Both of these sources give 9:30 A.M. as the recorded time of birth.

According to my rectification calculations, Marilyn's prenatal epoch (exchange between Ascendant/Descendant and the birth Moon, nine months previous to birth) is on August 31, 1925, at 5:22:24 P.M. PST in Los Angeles, CA (see Chart 39). This date yields a female epoch showing 19°07' Aquarius on the Ascendant, which is also her natal Moon's position. The Moon occupies 13°26' Aquarius, occupying the opposite sign and degree of her natal Leo Ascendant. The epoch Sun is at 8°05' Virgo. By Bailey's rules of rectification, this epoch is of the 2nd order (Irregular, 1st Variation) since her Moon at birth is above the horizon and decreasing in light, indicating a gestation period of more than 273 days.

The female epoch described above, sometimes defined as the conception chart, indicates that Marilyn's birth time should be rectified by adding one minute and forty-five seconds to the given time, making her rectified birth time 9:31:45 A.M. PST (see Chart 40). If this epoch is accepted as correct, Marilyn's rectified natal Ascendant is at 13°26' Leo and her Midheaven is at 6°27' Taurus. Natal Sun is at 10°27' Gemini; the Moon is at 19°07' Aquarius.

We have a reliable birth time to begin with, so this correction of less than two minutes brings it within the probable half-hour range for this type of rectification. If this rectified time of 9:32 A.M. (rounded) is accurate, the corresponding chart should respond to progressions and transits. Let's check it with important events in her life. Marilyn's three marriages have been selected as important events to confirm the rectified chart.

At age sixteen, Marilyn married Jim Dougherty. This marriage ended in divorce three years later. Their partnership was reported to have been "a marriage of convenience," typical of the planet Saturn. Despite her

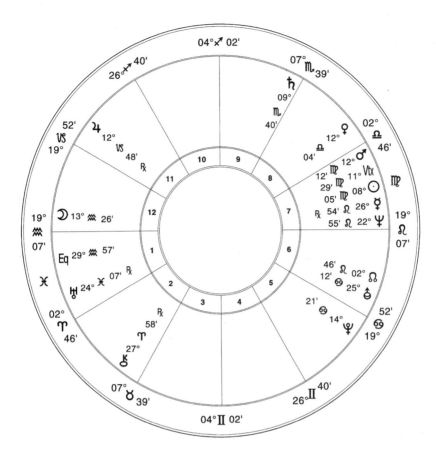

Chart 39. Marilyn Monroe's prenatal epoch, August 31, 1925, 5:22:24 P.M. PST, Los Angeles, CA, 118W15, 34N03. Source: Edna Rowland's rectification based on E.H. Bailey's rules; see above.

youth, Marilyn's foster parents and guardians urged her to marry.

Let's examine the secondary progressions for their wedding. Marilyn married Dougherty on June 19, 1942, when her progressed MC had reached 22° Taurus, squaring natal Neptune and opposing Saturn. A progressed aspect to the natal 7th house ruler is common when a marriage occurs. Saturn and Uranus are co-rulers of Marilyn's 7th house, so this opposition aspect between her progressed MC and Saturn is acceptable.

Marilyn's second marriage to New York Yankee outfielder, Joe DiMaggio, took place on January 14, 1954, in San Francisco, California, when

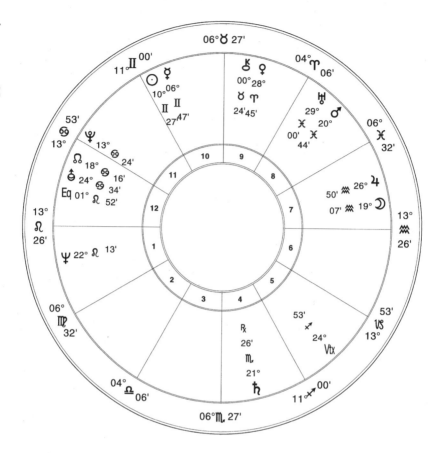

Chart 40. Marilyn Monroe's rectified birth chart. Born June 1, 1926, 9:31:45 A.M. PST, Los Angeles, CA, 118W15, 34N03. Source: Lois Rodden's Profiles of Women, page 81, cites 9:30 A.M. PST as the time given on the birth certificate. Rectification by Edna Rowland, by pre-natal method.

she was twenty-seven. The two met on a blind date while Marilyn was filming *Monkey Business*. He was divorced and had a twelve-year-old son. Although the marriage lasted only ten months, Marilyn and DiMaggio maintained a close, long-standing friendship throughout her short, tragic life. When she called on him, he responded promptly. Once, he even rescued her from a locked ward in a mental hospital. He made the funeral arrangements when she died, and dutifully sent red roses to her tomb every year on the anniversary of her death.

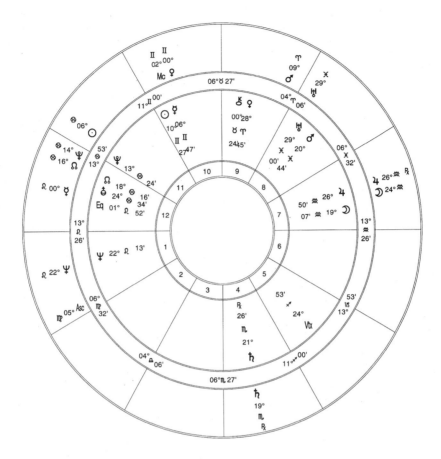

Chart 41. Monroe's rectified chart, progressed to Di Maggio marriage on January 14, 1954. Born June 1, 1926, 9:31:45 A.M. PST, Los Angeles, CA, 118W15, 34N03. Source: See Chart 40.

On the date of her marriage to Di Maggio (see Chart 41), Marilyn's progressed Moon at 24° Aquarius was in conjunction with her natal Moon/Jupiter midpoint in her Aquarian 7th house, and exactly sextile her natal Vertex. Her progressed MC at 2° Gemini was exactly opposite his Sun at 2° Sagittarius. Her progressed Equatorial Ascendant at 28° Leo was exactly inconjunct her natal 7th house ruler, Uranus, and trine her Venus at 28° Aries. Progressed Sun at 6° Cancer was exactly sesquiquadrate to her other 7th house ruler, Saturn; therefore, both of her 7th house rulers, Saturn and Uranus, were aspected by secondary progressions, as required by The Church of Light rectification formula for this event.

Now let's examine some of the synastry aspects between their birth charts. According to a current almanac, Joe DiMaggio was born November 25, 1914, in Martinez, California; hour of birth unknown. DiMaggio's natal Jupiter at 15° Aquarius closely conjoins Marilyn's Aquarius Moon in her 7th house, so he was inclined to be generous and overindulgent (Jupiter) to her needs. His own natal Moon (falling somewhere between 6-19° Pisces) near her Mars/Uranus (a widely separating conjunction) in her 8th house, spoils their compatibility. Uranus is friendly on a platonic level, but separative; and Mars, although passionate, is often a jealous and argumentative lover. DiMaggio's Moon at birth squares his natal Mars in 10° Sagittarius, repeating the disruptive pattern.

Astrological researcher Michel Gauquelin designates Mars as the ruling planet for professional sports champions. DiMaggio's Sun/Mars conjunction gave him the energy and strength needed to be a sports champion, but this aspect also bestows a quick temper, tending to make him impatient and impulsive. Marilyn herself has an erratic, disruptive natal Mars/Uranus conjunction in her 8th house, giving her similar qualities of impatience, impulsiveness, and temper on the negative side; but on the positive side, a beautiful and photogenic body. Before she became one of Hollywood's most glamorous stars, she was a model. Her nude calendar pose has now become a collector's item.

Marilyn's third and final marriage, to playwright Arthur Miller, lasted a full five years until they were divorced January 20, 1961. The marriage took place on June 29, 1956, after Miller's first wife granted him a long-awaited divorce. See Chart 42 for progressions to Marilyn's natal chart.

When Miller and Monroe were married in 1956, her progressed MC at 5° Gemini had reached a conjunction with her natal Sun-sign ruler, Mercury; progressed Mercury at 3° Leo was sextile progressed Venus. Marilyn's progressed Moon at 29° Pisces was exactly conjunct her natal and progressed Uranus (her 7th house ruler) at 29° Pisces. Her retrograde progressed Saturn was exactly square her Moon in the 7th. This takes care of the required progressed aspects to the 7th house rulers (Saturn and Uranus) at the time of the marriage partnership, so we can safe-

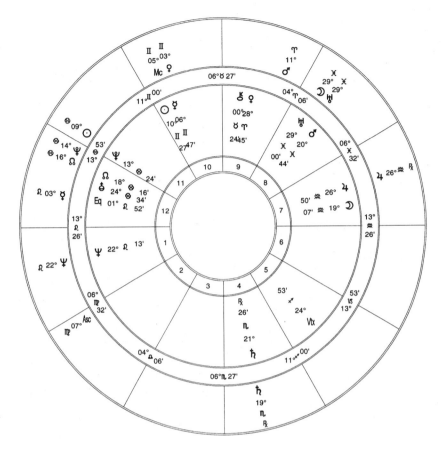

Chart 42. *Marilyn Monroe's rectified chart, progressed to Miller marriage, June 29, 1956. Born June 1, 1926, 9:31:45 A.M. PST, Los Angeles, CA, 118W15, 34N03. Source: Robert Slatzer's* The Life and Curious Death of Marilyn Monroe *for date of marriage.*

ly conclude the rectified time of birth is correct.

At age thirty, Marilyn's progressed Ascendant at 7° Virgo squared her natal 11th house ruler, Mercury, and opposed her natal 8th house cusp (surgery), so her hopes and wishes for having Miller's child were denied. During their five-year marriage, Marilyn experienced two ectopic pregnancies. In November 1958, she lost the second baby in the third month of her pregnancy. In June 1959, she had corrective surgery in hopes of having a child, but this was not to be. Instead, progressed retrograde Saturn at 19° Scorpio, exactly square her natal Moon and trine natal Mars in her 8th house of surgery, brought her two or three emergency stays in a hospital that almost cost her her life.

According to Rodden's *Astro Data II*, writer/dramatist Arthur Miller was born on October 17, 1915, at 5:12 A.M. EST, in New York City, New York. The source of this data is given as "C." Miller's best-known play was the Pulitzer prize-winning *Death of a Salesman*. After collaborating on *The Misfits* (1960), a play he wrote for Marilyn to star in, they divorced on the same day John F. Kennedy became president.

In comparing their charts and examining their mutual aspects, we note that Miller's Sun at 22° Libra exactly sextiles Marilyn's Neptune in her 1st house. His 11° Libra Ascendant closely sextiles her natal Ascendant at 13° Leo and trines her Sun, but his energy-draining South Node in Leo conjunct her natal Ascendant is unfortunate, especially so because his Uranus at 11° Aquarius opposes this point. They both had Moon in the same decan of Aquarius, closely conjunct, a rather compatible aspect. This Moon conjunction falls within his 5th house of children. Miller was forty when they married, and already had several children by a previous marriage, so he wasn't as anxious as she was to have a child. Since she was only thirty, he reluctantly went along with her plans.

During this period, Dr. Lee Siegel, Marilyn's Los Angeles physician, diagnosed her as having endometriosis (a condition where endometrial tissue, the mucous membrane lining of the uterus, can become displaced and inflamed). Tissue can adhere to the tubes, vagina, abdomen, and bladder, causing pain during intercourse and menstruation. The disease, while not life-threatening, is progressive, worsening with time, and the accumulated scar tissue often causes sterility. Since Marilyn refused to have a hysterectomy, the only known effective remedy for this disease in 1956, she was doomed to suffer and run the risk of life-threatening ectopic pregnancies. Her radical Moon at birth, ruling female functions and childbirth, received a close square from her 6th house ruler, Saturn, and the Moon, Saturn, and Neptune (her 8th house ruler) are all part of a Fixed T-square.

There were attempts to play down the publicity following her hospitalizations for this condition. Over time, she was becoming progressively addicted to painkilling drugs. She also suffered from insomnia, so doctors constantly prescribed barbiturates to help her sleep. As she gradually became dependent on the pills, she slipped into despondency and depression. Note her natal Saturn square Moon and Ascendant; this is a double indication of severe mood changes with periods of extreme depression (Saturn) and exhaustion. The South Node in Capricorn, a Saturn-ruled sign, on the cusp of her 6th house of health, didn't help either. In desperation, she frequently turned to doctors and tended to be overawed by their aura of authority.

During one of her last films, *The Misfits*, she was taking twenty pills a day, according to director, John Huston. Natal Neptune in 22° Leo in her 1st house closely squares Saturn at 21° Scorpio in her 4th house of endings and death; her overuse of drugs and alcohol (Neptune) was no secret, and no doubt greatly contributed to her eventual demise. Most authorities agree that she died from an overdose of Nembutal; but there is some doubt about how these pills were administered. In his book, *The Marilyn Conspiracy*, Milo Speriglio suggests the fatal dose may have been given by injection or enema, and he comes right out and voices his opinion that she was probably murdered. Dr. Thomas Noguchi with the Los Angeles coroner's office dubbed her death a "probable suicide," leaving room for legitimate doubt.

On July 31, 1962, just four days before Marilyn's tragic death, there was a Solar Eclipse at 7°49' Leo in her 12th house of self-undoing and secrets; this eclipse point squared her natal 10th and 4th house cusps, semi-squared her progressed Moon, and exactly opposed her progressed Vertex at 7°32' Aquarius. Further calculation for the Arabic *Part of Murder* (see Appendix) yields 7°29' Aquarius, which conjuncts her progressed Vertex and opposes the eclipse point. On the date of her death, transiting Saturn was conjunct the South Node at 8° Aquarius, also opposing the eclipse point. Obviously, the emphasis on these sensitive degrees is quite heavy!

According to my astrological calculations, Marilyn probably died at 11:46:11 P.M. PDT on Saturday, August 4, 1962, in Brentwood, California. Let's examine the event chart (see Chart 38) for the time of death, and the transits to her natal planets. At this time, the exact degree of her natal 4th house cusp (6°27' Scorpio) occupies the Descendant of her death chart; 21°27' Capricorn is the transiting MC. Transiting Sun, her Ascendant ruler

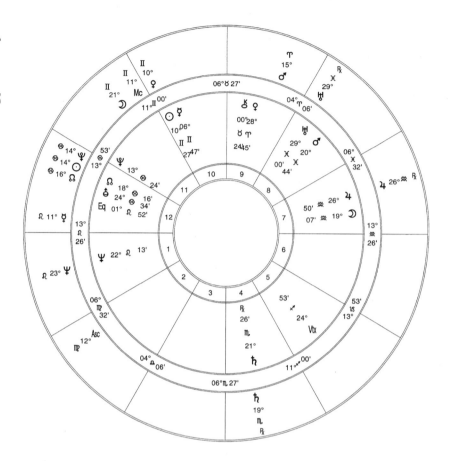

Chart 43. Marilyn Monroe's rectified birth chart, progressed to her death on August 4, 1962. Born June 1, 1926, 9:31:45 A.M. PST, Los Angeles, CA, 118W15, 34N03. Source: See Chart 38.

at 12° Leo on August 4th, is applying to a conjunction with her natal Ascendant. The transiting Sun also conjoins progressed Mercury, her Sun-sign ruler. Marilyn's natal Mars/Saturn (death) midpoint at 21° Capricorn is exactly conjunct the Midheaven on the death chart. On August 4, 1962, at 11:46 P.M. PDT, transiting Pluto at 8° Virgo was exactly conjunct Marilyn's prenatal epoch Sun, and conjunct the transiting Sun/Moon midpoint.

According to the precepts of Uranian astrology, Mars/Pluto aspects relate to the potential for murder or violent death; these two planets are co-rulers of her natal Scorpio 4th house of endings. Is it just a coincidence that Marilyn's 4th house cusp at 6°27' Scorpio occupies the 7th house cusp of her death chart and opposes Robert Kennedy's natal Ascendant at 6° Taurus? Was it only a rumor that he visited her home in Brentwood that evening just before her death, and may have been one of the last people to see her alive?

See Chart 43 for Marilyn's secondary progressions on the date of her death. Progressed Mars at 15° Aries is separating from a square to her progressed Sun/Pluto conjunction at 14° Cancer in her 12th house of self-undoing and secret enemies.

Calculations for an event chart of death emphasize the importance of the angles for rectification work. A few rules for rectification of the angles have been developed (see Preface) and can be repeated here, as follows:

In cases of violent death from unnatural causes, such as murder or public execution, the natal 10th or 7th house cusp may be rising at the time of death, especially if the death is followed by much publicity. The 10th and 7th house cusps are public houses, being *above* the horizon, whereas the 7th house rules open enemies, as well as all types of partnerships.

In most cases of suicide, however, the natal Ascendant degree or 1st house sign is usually rising at the time of death, indicating an act of self-destruction or a self-inflicted death. In Marilyn's case, this didn't happen, leading me to believe that she may have been murdered. Why, and by whom, is still open to question; but the timing of her death does leave many questions unanswered.

Based on application of these rectification rules (reversed, in this case, since we know the time of birth is accurate and we are seeking to estimate the exact time of death), I submit my theory that Marilyn's death was probably not suicide. During the period of 9:00 P.M. to 12:00 P.M. PDT—the possible period when the actress must have expired—the only possible birth chart angle *rising* was the 10th house natal angle, or 6° Taurus. This places her natal 4th house angle on the 7th house cusp of the death chart at 11:46:11 P.M. PDT for Brentwood, California.

If she did, indeed, commit suicide, the angle more likely to be rising would be her natal Ascendant; but her Leo Ascendant doesn't rise on August 4, 1962, in the P.M. at all! Instead, her Ascendant degree at 13°26'

Leo rises in the morning at about 6:25 A.M. on August 4th, and a little earlier, at 6:22 A.M. on the following day, August 5th.

To sum up, Marilyn was reportedly very much alive around 8 P.M. on August 4th, when she retired for the night, but when the police arrived between 4:45 A.M. and 5:00 A.M. the next morning, Sunday, August 5th, she had been dead several hours. The actress was dead by the time of the first call to police at 4:35 A.M. (August 5th), but the housekeeper states she found Marilyn dead in her bed shortly after midnight. The interval between midnight and 4:35 A.M. remains a mystery, as does the interval between 8:00 P.M. and midnight of August 4th, unless we accept the idea that Mrs. Murray may have found Marilyn's body just fifteen or twenty minutes after she died, around 11:46 P.M. This estimated time fits with the housekeeper's statements to the police when she was *first* questioned; but Mrs. Murray later changed her story, giving 3:30 A.M. as the time when she discovered the body.

The event chart for Marilyn's death, and corresponding aspects to her natal and progressed planets on August 4, 1962, suggest she may have met with foul play or that her death may have been accidental. There's no doubt she was suicidal; she had attempted to take her own life several times before. Because her death was accompanied by newspaper headlines and media publicity (10th house), and has been followed by a great deal of controversy about whether or not she was murdered, the rising of her 10th house natal cusp (6°27' Taurus) at the time of her death seems appropriate. The last word on her death has yet to be written, despite all the biographies and articles that appear about her.

In her book *From Reverence to Rape*, well-known film critic Molly Haskell has this to say about Marilyn, "Her suicide, as suicides do, casts a retrospective light on her life. Her ending gives her a beginning and a middle, turns her into a work of art with a message and a meaning." I couldn't agree more.

Epilogue

According to official police reports, Marilyn retired about 8:00 P.M. on Saturday, August 4, 1962. The coroner reported the time of death as 3:40 A.M. on Sunday, August 5th, while the police, being uncertain, reported the time of death as being between 8:00 P.M. on Saturday, August 4th, when Marilyn retired for the night, and 3:35 A.M. on Sunday, August 5th, an hour before Dr Engelberg called to report the death. Even the authorities couldn't agree on the facts as presented to them!

For those who would like to do additional research and/or chart comparisons, I include the following birth data for some of the people who were near Marilyn on the day she died.

1. Mrs. Eunice Murray, Marilyn's housekeeper, was born March 3, 1902, in Chicago, Illinois(deceased).

2. Dr. Ralph R. Greenson, Marilyn's psychiatrist, was born August 20, 1911, in Brooklyn, New York (deceased).

3. Margot Patricia Newcomb, Marilyn's press agent, was born July 9, 1930, in Washington, D.C.

4. Robert Kennedy was born November 20, 1925, at 3:11 P.M. EST in Brookline, Massachusetts (source: Rodden's *Astro Data III*; deceased).

Upon her death, the thirty-six-year-old actress left the bulk of her estate to the Strasbergs, who were her drama coaches and instructors, and her half-sister, Bernice Miracle. In her will, she also allotted a large portion of her estate for the lifetime care and guardianship of her mother, Gladys Pearl Monroe, who was mentally ill and required constant care and hospitalization. Her mother was born May 24, 1900, in Diaz, Mexico, and worked as a film cutter.

In 1982, the Los Angeles County prosecutor and then District Attorney John Van deKamp, decided to reopen the Monroe case for a criminal investigation. The team assigned to the case worked for four months and failed to come up with evidence to prove Marilyn died by any other means than that listed in the autopsy report. However, according to investigative reporter, George Carpozi, Jr., none of the four pathologists who studied Naguchi's initial findings agreed that Monroe died the way the autopsy indicated, and Dr. Naguchi, the coroner, stated: "If I had to do this autopsy over again, I would not have done it the way I had; I would have been much more thorough." And so, the mystery remains.

AP/ Wide World Photos

Chapter Ten

The Life and Death of Sylvia Plath

Sylvia Plath, American poet and writer, best known for her semi-autobiography, *The Bell Jar*, was born on October 27, 1932, in Boston, Massachusetts, to Otto Plath and Aurelia Schober. Otto Plath was a science professor at Boston University

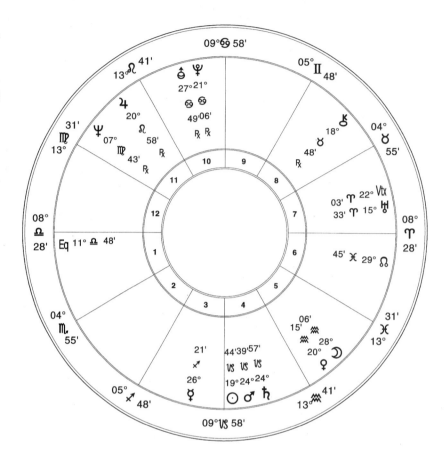

Chart 44. Sylvia Plath's prenatal epoch. January 10, 1932, 11:09:46 P.M. EST, Boston, MA, 71W04, 42N22. Placidus houses. Source: Calculation by Edna Rowland (see below).

when he met Aurelia, a student who became his wife in 1932. They were to have two children; Sylvia, and her younger brother, Warren.

According to Lois Rodden's *Profiles of Women*, Sylvia Plath was born at 2:10 P.M. EST; the time is from her birth certificate. Sylvia's prenatal epoch falls on January 10, 1932, at 11:09:46 P.M. EST (see Chart 44). The epoch chart shows the Moon's sign and degree at birth, 8° 28' Libra rising, and the epoch Moon at 28° 06' Aquarius (her Ascendant sign and degree at birth). Accordingly, I have corrected her birth time, resulting in a rectified birth time of 2:06:55 P.M. EST.

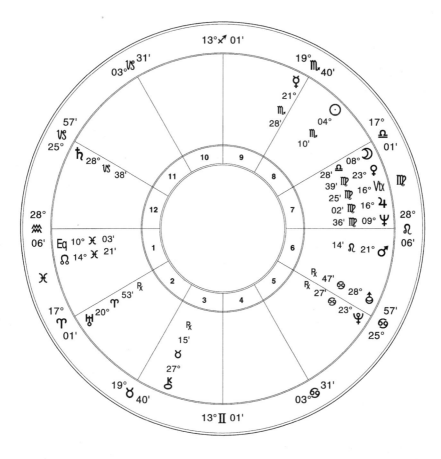

Chart 45. *Sylvia Plath's rectified birth chart. Born October 27, 1932, 2:06:55 P.M. EST, Boston, MA, 71W04, 42N22. Source: Lois Rodden's Profiles of Women, page 218, cites 2:10 P.M. EST. This chart is rectified to 3 minutes earlier by Edna Rowland, based on the prenatal epoch; see Chart 44.*

Sylvia's rectified birth chart (see Chart 45) shows her natal Moon in 8° Libra, 24 degrees behind her 4° Scorpio Sun (Dark Moon or Balsamic phase). She has 28°06' Aquarius on the Ascendant and a Midheaven of 13°01' Sagittarius. Her Ascendant ruler, Uranus, is at 20° Aries and retrograde; Saturn, co-ruler of her Ascendant, is positioned at 28° Capricorn in her 12th house. Since Pisces is intercepted in the 1st house, Neptune must also be considered a co-ruler of her Ascendant; this nebulous planet occupies 9° Virgo and falls in her 7th house. This unusual pattern of multiple co-rulership of her Ascendant certainly adds up to a rather complex personality. According to her biographers, Sylvia has been described very differently by various people who knew her during her short life span.

One month after the publication of *The Bell Jar* in 1963, Sylvia Plath committed suicide. She died in London, England on February 11, 1963, just three months after her thirtieth birthday. The manner of her death, and a previous suicide attempt, will be discussed in detail later.

Sylvia Plath's acquaintance with sorrow started early. Her world was shattered when her father, whom she adored, died in 1940, when she was only eight. Her father, Otto Plath, was born April 3, 1883, in Grabow, Poland. His unexpected death was the result of his stubborn refusal to consult a doctor until it was too late. He died at 9:35 P.M. on November 5, 1940, from complications following a leg injury and amputation on October 12, 1940.

Secondary progressions to Sylvia's rectified birth chart for the date of her father's death show the progressed MC at 21° Sagittarius, exactly trine natal Mars and conjoining her Mars/Uranus (accident) midpoint (see Chart 46). The progressed MC semisextiles natal Mercury at 21° Scorpio and squares the progressed Vertex at 22° Virgo.

Sylvia's progressed Ascendant at 12° Pisces squares the natal 4th house cusp of endings, and trines progressed Sun (the male parent) in her 8th house of death. The progressed Sun at 12° Scorpio is inconjunct her natal (Gemini) 4th house cusp. In a female chart, the 4th house and its occupants and rulers signify the father. The progressed Ascendant opposes progressed South Node and conjoins her Jupiter-Neptune midpoint, as well. The progressed Moon at 6° Aquarius occupies her 12th house of sorrows, semisquares the progressed MC, and is sesquiquadrate her progressed Vertex. Progressed Midheaven trines her natal and progressed Uranus (abrupt endings) at 20° Aries, confirming the suddenness of the event.

Because her father's death (natal Saturn opposite Pluto) was so sudden and unexpected (Uranus), she may have found the loss difficult, and her youth would have made it doubly hard to accept. Her chart emphasizes the importance of this event in her life. At birth, her ruler, Uranus, squares Saturn and Pluto, and is inconjunct Mercury, the 4th house ruler

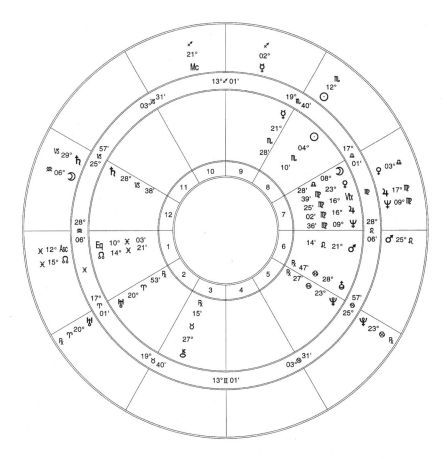

Chart 46. *Sylvia Plath's rectified chart progressed to her father's death on November 5, 1940. Born October 27, 1932, 2:06:55 P.M. EST, Boston, MA, 71W04, 42N22. Placidus houses. Source:* Sylvia Plath: Method and Madness *by Edward Burschor.*

representing the father. Natal Mercury squares Mars exactly (unresolved anger), and is sextile Saturn and trine Pluto.

Six months after her father's death, Sylvia's first poem was published in the *Boston Sunday Herald.* Her mother obtained a much-needed teaching position, and the family moved to Wellesley, Massachusetts, where Sylvia spent the remainder of her childhood until she left for Smith College at age eighteen. With an IQ of 160, it wasn't difficult for this young woman to win a scholarship to college in Northampton where she majored in English. Later on, she won a Fulbright Fellowship to Cambridge University, where she met her future husband, poet Ted Hughes. The two were to become the major British and American poets of their era.

The youngest of three children, Edward "Ted" Hughes, was born on August 17, 1930, in a small town called Mytholmroyd in Yorkshire, England. Sylvia and Ted eloped while they were attending Cambridge together. They tried, unsuccessfully, to keep their marriage a secret since they were close to graduation and feared it might interfere with their scholarships. They were married in London on June 16, 1956.

Let's compare the birth charts of the marriage partners to judge their compatibility, or lack of it. (Since Ted's birth time is unknown, a sunrise chart will have to suffice.) Ted's Sun at 23° Leo is conjunct Sylvia's natal Mars at 21° Leo, falling near the cusp of her 7th house of marriage. This mutual Sun/Mars aspect assures us there was no lack of excitement or physical compatibility on a sexual level within this union, but the potential for frequent disagreements and violent quarrels is also indicated by the strength of this Mars conjunction. Ted's Leo Sun closely squares Sylvia's Mercury, triggering her natal Mercury square Mars, which is an argumentative aspect.

Ted's natal Venus at 7° Libra, almost exactly conjunct Sylvia's Moon at 8° Libra, is undoubtedly the aspect that brought these two together and held them together for some time. Moon/Venus aspects add a bit of tenderness and sentimentality, and are often found between lovers. This is probably the most favorable aspect between their charts. Falling as it does within Sylvia's 7th house, it promises marriage. However, Ted's natal Venus/Saturn square (misunderstandings) indicates a tendency toward selfishness and excessive egotism in love, and their favorable Moon/Venus conjunction is squared by his natal Saturn at 5° Capricorn, spoiling the promised compatibility to some extent.

According to Plath's biographer, Linda Martin, Ted was known to have indulged in a love affair with another woman during the latter part of their disintegrating marriage. Sylvia was evidently aware of this affair, but persisted in the relationship, hoping for a reconciliation. By 1963, the couple was estranged and living apart, although they were still officially married at the time of Sylvia's death.

Chart 47. Progression of Sylvia Plath's rectified birth chart to the date of her marriage to Ted Hughes, June 16, 1956. Born October 27, 1932, 2:06:53 P.M. EST, Boston, MA, 71W04, 42N22. Placidus houses. Source: Sylvia Plath: A Biography by Linda W. Martin.

Ted's Moon in Taurus widely opposes Sylvia's natal Sun in Scorpio, and this, too, is an aspect that suggests marriage. According to psychiatrist Carl Jung's statistics, the aspect is usually considered more harmonious if the man's Sun conjoins or opposes the woman's Moon, rather than vice versa. Nevertheless, the Sun/Moon aspect indicates that Ted and Sylvia complemented each other. Ted's Mars squares Sylvia's Venus, indicating that attraction and excitement filled the air when they met.

Unfortunately, when they married on June 16, 1956, Sylvia's progressed MC at 6° Capricorn was conjunct Ted's natal Saturn and square his natal Venus, activating his natal Venus/Saturn square; see Chart 47. At age twenty-three, Sylvia's progressed MC was square her progressed Vertex, semisquare natal Mercury, sesquiquadrate natal Mars, and conjunct her Venus-Uranus midpoint. Her progressed Ascendant at 13° Aries was sesquiquadrate her progressed Sun at 27° Scorpio.

Sylvia's progressed Sun, ruler of her 7th house of marriage, was at the zenith of her chart, squaring both her natal Ascendant and Descendant, and sextile natal Saturn. The Sun's sextile to Saturn seems to confirm the initial secrecy surrounding the marriage, since Saturn occupied her natal 12th house of behind-the-scenes activity. Progressed Mercury at 19° Sagittarius semisquares her natal Sun in 4° Scorpio. It was only natural that she would be attracted to a Leo man; the Aquarius/Leo polarity on her natal horizon made this a probable choice. During their marriage, which lasted six years, they had two children, a boy and a girl.

At the time of their marriage, Ted was just two months away from his twenty-sixth birthday. His progressed Moon was getting ready to make its twenty-seven-year lunar return, but in June of 1956, it was still in the 1st decan of Taurus in opposition to Sylvia's natal Sun in Scorpio. This repeated the natal Moon-Sun opposition between their charts, described earlier. Ted's progressed Venus in 4° Scorpio conjoins Sylvia's natal Sun in 4° Scorpio, assuring temporary affinity and a bond of mutual interest while the progressed conjunction lasted.

Ted's progressed MC at 3° Gemini squares his natal Neptune (infatuation). Sylvia's progressed Mars at the time of the marriage occupies 3° Virgo, squaring Ted's progressed MC and conjunct his natal Neptune. Ted's progressed Mars at 8° Cancer activates his unfortunate natal Venus/Saturn square, and progressed Mercury at 6° Libra completes this cardinal T-square, as it conjoins his natal Venus. Ted's progressed Ascendant at 10° Virgo conjuncts Sylvia's angular Neptune in her 7th house of marriage; Neptune in her 7th house suggests excessive idealism and a strong inner emotional dependence on the partner. These mutual Neptune aspects indicate the potential for deep infatuation, deception, and eventual betrayal. With Neptune things are not quite what they seem to be. Neptune also encourages both parties to play the martyr and indulge in self-pity.

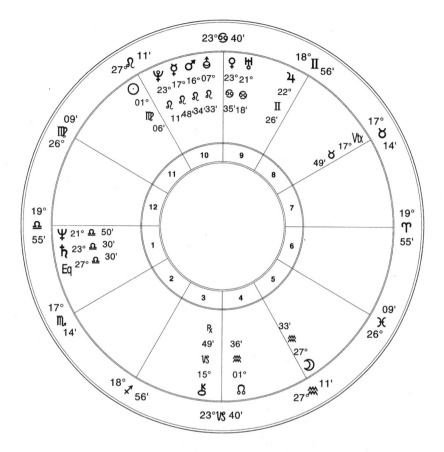

Chart 48. Event chart for attempted suicide. Date: August 24, 1953, 9:17 A.M. EST, Welles-ley, MA, 71W17, 42N18. Source: Sylvia Plath: Method and Madness by Edward Burschor.

Since Neptune rules the intercepted sign, Pisces, in Sylvia's natal 1st house, aspects to this planet are doubly important to her, affecting her personally. Sylvia's Ascendant on the cusp of Aquarius/Pisces combines the personality traits of both signs. At her birth, Neptune occupied her natal Saturn/Uranus midpoint. Ebertin describes this occupied midpoint or "tree"in these words: "The inability to face emotional stresses, falsehood or malice caused through weakness. A resolve to resign oneself to the inevitable, the abandonment of resistance, weakening strength, separation, mourning and bereavement."

No doubt Sylvia's separation from her husband in the latter part of 1962 contributed greatly to her final decision to commit suicide. So did her illness and depressed state of mind. In all fairness to both parties, I must add that Sylvia had, indeed, been suicidal and subject to severe bouts of depression (Saturn in the 12th opposite Pluto) long before she met and married Ted Hughes. Saturn-Pluto people often feel persecuted, even when there is no objective reason for their feelings.

At 9:17 A.M. EST on August 24, 1953, when Sylvia was twenty (see Chart 48), she made an unsuccessful attempt to kill herself by swallowing forty-eight sleeping pills. She hid in a crawl space in the basement of her parent's home in Wellesley, Massachusetts. Her grandmother found her on August 26, 1953, when she went down to the basement to do the family laundry and heard her moans. Sylvia, who had been missing for two days and was almost dead, was rushed to a hospital. After a partial recovery, she was committed to a state mental institution where she underwent electric shock therapy. Six months later, she was released and went home.

From that time on, she lived with secret fears of a recurrence of the illness (Saturn in the 12th house of institutions and hospitals), although she struggled courageously with bouts of depression throughout her short but active life. At the time of her attempted suicide, transiting Venus (Sylvia's 8th house ruler) was exactly conjunct natal Pluto at 23° Cancer and square transiting Saturn at 23° Libra. Neptune conjuncts the Libra Ascendant and transiting Venus is conjunct the Midheaven at 23° Cancer; Venus squares both Neptune and Saturn. Transiting Neptune is conjunct Sylvia's natal Sun/Moon midpoint. The Sun/Moon midpoint is an important point often called the second Ascendant. Transiting Sun at 1° Virgo is exactly conjunct progressed Mars and conjunct her natal Mars/Neptune midpoint. Her choice of sleeping pills as the instrument of death is indicated by Neptune since this planet rules drugs, including barbiturates. As previously explained in Chapter 9, women who commit suicide usually prefer to use non-disfiguring, less violent methods than men.

Plath's *final* suicide attempt was successful in the early morning hours of February 11, 1963, probably sometime between 6:00 A.M. and 9:30 A.M. She was residing in London with her two children and seriously contemplating obtaining a divorce from Ted, who was by now living with

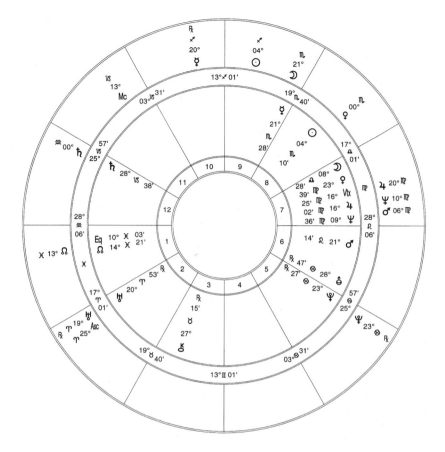

Chart 49. *Progression of Sylvia Plath's rectified birth chart to the date of her suicide on February 11, 1963. Born October 27, 1932, 2:06:55 P.M. EST, Boston, MA, 71W04, 42N22. Placidus houses. Source: Sylvia Plath: A Biography by Linda W. Martin.*

another woman. It was on this fateful night that she made her final decision. After putting the children to sleep and ensuring their safety, Sylvia
took a few leftover sleeping pills and put her head into the gas oven in the
kitchen. Sylvia and the children had been ill, so a nurse had been hired to
help with their care. At about 9:30 A.M., the nurse arrived at the house and
found her dead. An inquest the next day ruled her death a suicide.

Chart 49 shows the progressions on the date of her death: Progressed
MC at 13° Capricorn trines her natal Nodes; the progressed Ascendant
at 25° Aries conjoins her Saturn/Pluto midpoint. The description of this

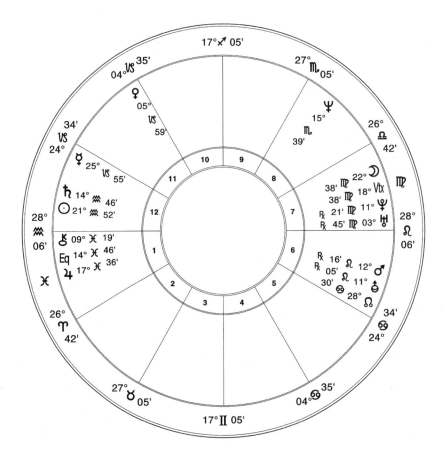

Chart 50. Plath's estimated death chart, rectified by the author. Date: February 11, 1963, 7:41:55 A.M. GMT, London, England, 0W10, 51N30. Source: Sylvia Plath: A Biography by Linda Martin (which provides only the appropriate time interval for her death).

direct or occupied midpoint by Ebertin in *The Combination of Stellar Influences* is aptly appropriate: "Emplacement in cumbersome and difficult circumstances. Separation, mourning and bereavement."

The *Part of Suicide* (see Appendix for calculations), at 5°31' Aries, falls in her 1st house, inconjunct the Sun in her 8th house, and opposite her natal Moon in Libra. On further examination of the progressions for February 11, 1963, Sylvia's thirtieth year, we note that the Sun has progressed to 4°38' Sagittarius in trine to the Part of Suicide. Progressed

Mars at 6° Virgo in her 7th house (indicating quarrels with the spouse) is inconjunct the Suicide Part, and the Progressed Moon at 21° Scorpio is in a sesquiquadrate aspect to this point. Natal Mercury, ruler of her 4th house of endings, at 21° Scorpio is also making a sesquiquadrate aspect to the Suicide Point, and so is her natal Mars at 21° Leo in her 6th house of illness and servants. The natal Mars aspect, referring as it does to the 6th house of servants, probably indicates the presence of the nurse who discovered Sylvia's body.

I believe Sylvia actually died at 7:42 GMT on the morning of February 11th, since her natal Ascendant of 28°06' Aquarius was rising at this time. This fits the time-of-death formula for suicides (requiring the rising sign at birth to become the 1st house cusp of the death chart so that the death and natal charts mirror each other). It's also within the known time limits of her death, 6:00 A.M. to 9:30 A.M. as reported by the authorities.

Chart 50, for the time of death, shows progressed Mercury, Sylvia's 4th house ruler, in the 10th aspecting the Midheaven, squaring the Vertex, and opposing the 4th house cusp. Transiting Jupiter (ruler of her natal 10th house) at 17° Pisces forms an opposition aspect to her natal Jupiter at 16° Virgo. It exactly squares the 4th and 10th houses of the death chart (17° Gemini/Sagittarius), *repeating* the natal Jupiter square to these house cusps which existed when she was born!

The polarity between these parental angles has already been explained. In Sylvia Plath's era, women were still struggling valiantly with conflicts between career interests (10th house) and home life (4th house). To challenge these conventional concepts was to directly challenge society and be known as a rebel (Uranus). Whether intentionally or not, with her Ascendant ruler, Uranus, in 20° Aries trine Mars at birth, and square her Sun sign ruler, Pluto, Sylvia Plath was more than adequately prepared to do just that! Aquarians are often born before their time.

The following transits on the date of her death are even more significant, amplifying the progressions: Transiting Pluto at 11° Virgo opposes Sylvia's natal East Point (EP) and conjuncts her natal Neptune. Transiting Sun at 21° Aquarius exactly opposes her natal Mars in her natal 6th house, and transiting Venus at 5° Capricorn is exactly square the *Part of Suicide*. Transiting Neptune at 15° Scorpio is in her natal 8th house, indicating the mode of death as asphyxiation by gas fumes, and transiting Mercury at 25° Capricorn forms an opposition to her natal Pluto at 23° Cancer.

In Chapter 9, I described death by gas fumes as relating to afflictions to Saturn, especially from Mercury and Pluto. Does Sylvia's chart fulfill these requirements? Let's see.

In examining her birth chart, we see natal Saturn occupies 28° Capricorn and is conjunct transiting Mercury and the South Node at the time of her death. Also mentioned in reference to asphyxiation are the 13th degree of the Mutable signs and a progressed aspect to Neptune (gas). Sylvia's 4th house cusp (IC) at birth is 13° Gemini. It was receiving a progressed inconjunct aspect from Neptune (gas) at her death, so the prescribed rules are fulfilled. Chapter 9 also describes how women tend to be most negatively affected by the failure or breakdown of important intimate relationships. This is a common cause for female suicide. Unfortunately, with Neptune in her 7th house conjunct her prenatal eclipse point, together with her generational bias, Sylvia may have felt that her survival depended on her marriage partner.

The publication of Sylvia's semi-autobiography, *The Bell Jar*, shortly before her death at age thirty, apparently only served to deepen her depression (Saturn) rather than mitigate it. Was she afraid of success? Weakened physically by recurring bouts of flu (Progressed Moon square Mars), and worried about dwindling finances, she finally succumbed in the face of her suffering to embrace the final escape—death.

Ironically, fame quickly followed her demise. *The Colossus*, one of her most quoted poems, and many other volumes of her poetry, now adorn library shelves all over the world. Feeling rejected by life, this Scorpio native was lovingly accepted in death.

Epilogue

Sylvia had two children. Frieda Rebecca Hughes was born on April 1, 1960, at 5:45 A.M. GMT in London, England. Her son, Nicholas Farrar Hughes, was a healthy ten pounds at birth. He was born in London, England on January 17, 1962, at 11:55 P.M. Both children were delivered at Plath's home, with a midwife assisting. Their birth data was obtained from Edward Butscher's book, *Sylvia Plath: Method and Madness*.

Frieda grew up to become a painter and writer; Nicholas became a marine biologist, most recently working in Alaska.

Midpoints Associated with Violence or Homicide

The following planetary midpoints may be strongly emphasized when murder, suicide, or violent accidents occur, but they are not significant by themselves; they must be activated by a third planet. This third planet, which forms a tree pattern, may be either a natal, progressed, or transiting planet. This is sometimes called an "occupied," or direct, midpoint.

Don't be alarmed if you have natal planets occupying some of the degrees mentioned in these appendices, or even several of these degrees. The entire chart must be examined carefully, and natal, progressed, or transiting planets must all repeat any violent aspects or midpoints many times before an astrologer is justified in predicting the possibility of danger or violence. Other factors such as house positions of planets and aspects must also be evaluated for severe afflictions involving several planets in these sensitive areas.

Although many birth charts probably contain some planets activating these sensitive degrees, this isn't considered significant unless accompanied by other corroborating factors. Sometimes the negative influences are only temporary, as indicated by fast-moving transits of inner planets to natal or progressed planets. Many people in the helping professions, such as police officers, social workers, psychiatrists, and even fiction writers like Stephen King and Joyce Carol Oates (who write about murder), have planets in some of the so-called violent areas or degrees, but they have learned to direct these energies into positive channels.

The following midpoints have been found to be occupied or activated most frequently when a crime of violence or an accident occurs:

Mars/Saturn. Death; tendency to get hurt or injured; pain and suffering from cruelty.

Mars/Pluto. Murder; brutality; extreme violence; ruthless aggression.

Saturn/Pluto. Murder; cruelty; likely to be neglected or deprived of essential needs.

Mars/Uranus. Accidents or sudden bodily injury; impulsive acts; neglect of safety; quick temper.

Jupiter/Saturn. Arrest. Dealings with the law or legal system. Dissatisfaction.

Mars/Neptune. Suffering from harm or exploitation; weakness or increased vulnerability. Allergies or craving for drugs.

Note that an orb of only one degree (and no more than two degrees) should be allowed either applying or separating to these midpoints or occupied degrees for natal or progressed planets. Transits may exceed these orb limits somewhat, but it's best to keep the smaller orb suggested above, especially for close rectification work. For further information and more detailed interpretation of midpoints, refer to *The Combination of Stellar Influences*, by Reinhold Ebertin, as well as Michael Munkasey's *Midpoints—Unleashing the Power of the Planets*.

Appendix 2

Seven Special-Interest Arabic Parts

1. *Part of Assassination* (A): Ascendant plus the ruler of the 12th house, minus Uranus. This part was formulated by Ivy M. Goldstein Jacobson.

2. *Part of Coma* (C): Ascendant plus Neptune, minus Saturn. This part was formulated by Doris V. Thompson.

3. *Part of Death* (D): Ascendant plus 8th house Cusp, minus Moon.

4. *Part of Imprisonment* (I): Ascendant plus Sun, minus Neptune.

5. *Part of Murder* (M): Mercury plus Saturn, minus Mars. Developed by an astrologer named Orion.

6. *Part of Rape* (R): Sun plus Neptune, minus Uranus. This part was formulated by WSA Research Group of California, headed by astrologer/director Jeannette Glenn.

7. *Part of Suicide* (S): Ascendant plus 8th house cusp, minus Neptune.

Glossary

activate

To move to activity.

adverse aspect

See "hard" under "aspect, modifying terms for."

afflict, afflicted, afflictions

Difficult or unfavorably aspected planets or houses. Usually refers to "hard" aspects such as the square, semisquare, inconjunct (mildly adverse), or sesquiquadrate, etc. May also refer to a planet or house with difficult, stressful aspects and little or no beneficial aspects to counteract the negativity.

Air signs

A triplicity of three signs: Gemini, Libra, and Aquarius.

angles

See "angular."

angular

The 1st, 4th, 7th, and 10th houses and planets therein. Sometimes called *angles*, since these cusps divide the four quadrants of the birth chart. Planets on or close to these cusps or angles are thought to strongly affect an individual.

applying

When a planet is approaching or going toward an exact degree or aspect with another planet, or house cusp, it is applying; the opposite of separating.

Aquarius

See "signs."

Aries

See "signs."

Ascendant

The zodiacal degree and sign on the eastern horizon (on the left-hand side of the chart) at the time of birth; sometimes called the *rising sign*.

aspect

The longitudinal distance between two planets, such as the square (90°), or the trine (120°), etc.

> **conjunct:** 0°.
> **inconjunct::** 150°.
> **opposition:** 180°.
> **semisextile:** 30°.
> **semisquare:** 150°.

sesquiquadrate: 135°.
sextile: 60°.
square: 90°.
trine: 120°.

aspect, modifying terms for

hard: Stressful or unfavorable aspects such as the square (90°), semisquare (45°), sesquiquadrate (135°), and inconjunct (150°) which is mildly adverse.

soft: Favorable aspects such as the trine (120°), sextile (60°), and semisextile (30°). The conjunction (0°) may or may not be considered beneficial depending on the planets and other factors involved.

astrology, types of

horary: A branch of astrology which has its own set of rules, and focuses on casting a chart for the moment a question is asked, or an event occurs.

mundane: Also called judicial or political astrology, as it is devoted to the study of planetary cycles or patterns that affect world events or politics, and forecasting future events.

natal: Genethliacal astrology, devoted to the study of the birth charts of individuals and their life and character.

"at home"

See "home sign."

Bacchus

Another name for Transpluto.

Balsamic Moon

A phase of the Moon or personality type as defined by astrologer Dane Rudhyar, classifying all persons born with the Moon less than 45° behind the Sun, or three-and-a-half days before the New Moon. Moon semisquare the Sun.

benefic

Usually refers to the planets Venus and Jupiter, when they are not afflicted by other factors.

birth chart

See "chart."

birth data

The month, date, year, birthplace (longitude and latitude), and hour of birth—the data necessary to erect an exactly timed natal birth chart.

Cancer

See "signs."

Capricorn

See "signs."

Cardinal

Refers to the common leadership and initiative qualities of the signs Aries, Cancer, Libra, and Capricorn.

challenging aspect

See "hard" under "aspect, modifying terms for." The negativity of this type of aspect is often difficult for the individual to overcome.

chart

In natal astrology also called a horoscope, radix, nativity, or birth chart, and usually refers to a chart erected for an individual based on the month, date, year, birthplace, and birth time. May refer to a progressed or transit chart for a timed event.

Chiron

A comet or planetoid (originally thought to have been a planet) discovered between Saturn and Uranus in 1977; it is described as "the wounded healer" and is a symbol of potential healing.

close aspect

Another way of saying that an aspect is nearly or almost exact. See "exact aspect."

conjunct, conjoined, conjunction

Within the same sign and degree of longitude. See "aspects."

co-ruling, co-ruler

A planet that shares rulership of a sign with another planet.

cosmobiologist

A member of the German cosmobiology movement, an empirical school of astrology founded by Reinhold Ebertin. A cosmobiologist is an astrologer who focuses mainly on the angularity and midpoints between two planets.

crossing

Passing over another planet or house cusp.

culminating

A planet above the horizon, usually in or near the 10th house cusp; also called an *elevated* planet.

cusp

The line dividing any two houses of the horoscope. For example, the line of the Ascendant marks the

1st house cusp, the next line marks the 2nd house cusp, etc.

cusp ruler

The planet ruling the sign on the cusp of the house.

cycle, Moon

In reference to secondary progressions, the twenty-seven-year cycle of the Moon refers to the Moon's return to its own natal sign and degree position.

cycle, Uranus

The opposition of Uranus to its natal position in a chart. This occurs between ages 42–47, depending on the natal position of Uranus and other factors. Uranus completes its cycle in 84 years.

decan, decanate

Each thirty-degree sign contains three decans of ten degrees each.

decreasing moon

Moon's waning phase lasting about two weeks from Full Moon to New Moon.

degree

One-360th of any circle. Some astrologers have assigned specific meanings to certain degrees, such as 18–19° Aries/Libra (a homicidal degree) or 8–9° Taurus (an alcoholic degree). In horary and natal astrology the 29th degree is regarded as a "critical degree" regardless of what sign it occupies.

Descendant

The opposite point or angle from the Ascendant; the 7th house cusp.

detriment

A planet occupying the opposite sign to the sign that it rules. For example, Venus rules Taurus, so Venus in Scorpio is considered to be in detriment.

dignify

A somewhat antiquated term used to describe the condition of a planet that is strengthened by either sign position (essential dignity) or house position (accidental dignity).

dispositor

Ruler of the sign another planet is located in. For example, if Mercury is in Taurus, Venus (Taurus' ruler) is said to be Mercury's dispositor.

diurnal

The apparent diurnal (daily) motion of the planets resulting from the axial rotation of the Earth.

dual sign

Refers to a "double-bodied" sign such as Gemini, Sagittarius, or Pisces.

Earth Signs

A triplicity of three signs: Taurus, Virgo, and Capricorn.

eastern horizon

The left-hand side of the chart.

East Point

See "Equatorial Ascendant."

eclipse

An astronomical phenomena involving the parallel conjunction of the Sun, Moon, and Earth. Solar eclipses occur on the New Moon; Lunar eclipses occur on the Full Moon.

ecliptic

The apparent, or elliptical, path of the sun, where eclipses occur.

elements

The four elemental substances Fire, Earth, Air, and Water.

elevated

A planet above the horizon, usually in or near the 10th house cusp; also called a *culminating* planet.

ephemeris

An astrologer's almanac containing the computed positions of the Sun, Moon, and planets for each day of the year, relative to a terrestrial observer.

Equatorial Ascendant

The East Point (EP), sometimes called the second Ascendant, since it is calculated from the equator rather than from the ecliptic. The point where the eastern horizon intersects the prime vertical and the celestial equator.

exact aspect

An aspect with no orb. Used loosely to refer to an aspect within a one-degree-or-less orb.

exaltation, exalted

Traditionally, a planet is said to be *exalted* by its position in a sign deemed more positive than the sign it rules.

falls on

Occupies the same place in a chart. Loosely used to mean conjoins or is conjunct to, within a certain orb.

favorable aspect

See "soft" under "aspect, modifying terms for."

Fire signs

A triplicity of three signs: Aries, Leo, and Sagittarius.

Fixed

Refers to the common steadfast qualities or characteristics of the signs Taurus, Leo, Scorpio, and Aquarius.

fixed star

A self-luminous celestial body, as distinguished from a planet that shines by reflected light.

focal planet

A planet that enters an empty space created by a T-square, either by transit or progression

Full Moon

The monthly or progressed phase of the Moon where the Sun and the Moon are in exact opposition (180° apart).

Gauquelin plus sector

Michel and Françoise Gauquelin's research defined certain areas of the horoscope as "Gauquelin plus sectors," attributing great importance to planets in these areas. Roughly, the area just past the eastern horizon (Ascendant) or upper meridian (Midheaven).

Gemini

See "signs."

geocentric

Earth-centered, in contrast to heliocentric, which is Sun-centered.

grand cross

See "grand square."

grand square

A challenging, stressful configuration composed of four planets, each one making squares, and an opposition to the other three planets.

> **Cardinal grand square:** A grand square composed of Cardinal planets.
>
> **Fixed grand square:** A grand square composed of Fixed planets.
>
> **Mutable grand square:** A grand square composed of Mutable planets.

grand trine

A configuration of three planets,

each 120° from the other, forming a triangle.

Fire grand trine: A grand trine composed of Fire planets.

Earth grand trine: A grand trine composed of Earth planets.

Air grand trine: A grand trine composed of Air planets.

Water grand trine: A grand trine composed of Water planets.

hard aspect

See "aspect, modifying terms for."

harmonious aspect

See "soft" under "aspect, modifying terms for."

home sign, "at home in"

A planet residing in a sign that it rules.

horary astrology

See "astrology, types of."

horizon

The horizontal line dividing the chart or circle into two sectors—upper and lower.

horoscope

See "chart."

house

There are twelve houses, roughly dividing the twenty-four-hour diurnal circle into approximately two hours for each house; they are numbered counterclockwise from the Ascendant. Each house has a distinct meaning. Houses may be equal or unequal in size, depending on the house system or method used to compute them. The following keywords are associated with the various houses. (See an astrology textbook for additional meanings.)

1st: Self, outer personality, physical characteristics.

2nd: Monetary gains, possessions. Value systems.

3rd: Siblings. Elementary school. Short trips.

4th: Home, childhood conditioning. Parents and heritage. End of life.

5th: Romantic love, children, and creative pursuits.

6th: Service to others, jobs, health.

7th: Marriage, partnerships of all types, public enemies.

8th: Death, inheritance. Sexual

preferences. Joint finances.

9th: Religious and philosophical beliefs. Legal matters. Foreign travel.

10th: Reputation. Profession and fame or publicity. Parents.

11th: Friendships, hopes, and wishes. Step-children or adopted children.

12th: Prisons. Hospitals. Self-undoing. Hidden enemies. Secrets.

house ruler

The planet that rules the sign on the cusp of the house, or a planet ruling an intercepted house. (However, planets within houses are also considered influential and may modify delineations accordingly.)

IC

Abbreviation for Imum Coeli. The point opposite the Midheaven or meridian; the fourth house cusp. (Not to be confused with the Nadir.)

inconjunct

See "aspect."

increasing moon

Moon's waxing phase lasting about two weeks from New Moon to Full Moon.

inharmonious aspect

See "hard" under "aspect, modifying terms for."

inner planets

Mercury, Venus, Mars, and Jupiter.

intercepted

Refers to more than one sign occupying a house, resulting in two successive houses with non-continuous signs on their house cusps. Most house systems, with the exception of the equal house system, utilize houses of various sizes.

Jupiter

See "planets."

Leo

See "signs."

Libra

See "signs."

lifecycle midpoint

The halfway point (or age) between the dates of life and death.

luminaries

The Sun and Moon. For convenience, astrologers may sometimes refer to the Sun and Moon as planets but the difference is clearly understood.

lunar Nodes

The Moon's Nodes—a point (not a planet) where the Moon passes the ecliptic, sometimes referred to as the Dragon's Head (North Node) and Dragon's Tail (South Node).

malefic

An antiquated term that applies to certain planets deemed to have a harmful or unfavorable influence, usually Mars and Saturn; but may also be loosely applied to an afflicted planet, or a conjunction with a malefic.

Mars

See "planets."

Mars/Pluto midpoint

See "midpoint."

Mars/Saturn midpoint

See "midpoint."

Mars/Uranus midpoint

See "midpoint."

Midheaven

Medium Coeli (MC); the 10th house cusp; the meridian of the birthplace.

midpoint

The halfway point between two planets, calculated by adding both planets' longitude, then halving this sum. The significance of a midpoint can be modified by any planet that conjoins the midpoint.

Mars/Pluto midpoint: Murder. Rage and/or revenge. Ruthless aggression. Violent sexual impulses. Power struggles.

Mars/Saturn midpoint: Death. Depression. Frustration or impotence.

Mars/Uranus midpoint: Accident-proneness. Risk-taking. Rebellion.

Moon/Saturn midpoint: Codependency—usually, but not always, parental. Maternal deprivation.

Saturn/Pluto midpoint: Cruelty or violent assault. Sadism. Inner compulsions or obsessions.

Sun/Pluto midpoint:Rape and/or homicide. Urge to

control. Manipulation.

Sun/Mars midpoint: Violence. Masculine aggression and virility. Assertiveness, likelihood to take action.

minor aspect

See "aspect."

Moon/Saturn midpoint

See "midpoint."

Moon

See "planets."

Mutable

Refers to the common flexible and adaptable qualities of the signs Gemini, Virgo, Sagittarius, and Pisces.

mutual reception

A helpful relationship between two planets, each of which occupies the other's sign of rulership or exaltation.

Nadir

The lowest point—the opposite of the Zenith. (Not to be confused with the IC.)

natal

Birth, as in natal chart.

native

Refers to the individual who owns the nativity, or birth chart.

natural cusp ruler

The planet that rules the corresponding sign that would be on the cusp if 0° Aries was the 1st house cusp (Ascendant). For example, Mercury is the *natural ruler* of the 3rd house because Mercury rules the 3rd sign, Gemini.

negative aspect

See "hard" under "aspect, modifying terms for."

Neptune

See "planets."

New Moon

A conjunction of the Sun and Moon. It may refer to a transit, progression, or natal configuration.

Nodes

See "lunar Nodes." There are other planetary nodes besides those of the Moon, but they are referred to rarely.

North Node

See "lunar Nodes."

occupied midpoint

See "midpoint." When planets occupy the empty space on either side of the midpoint it is sometimes called a *tree* or *planetary picture* by cosmobiologists.

opposed, opposing, opposition

See "aspect."

orb

The area of effective influence for an aspect. Progressions require small orbs—usually one degree on either side of an exact aspect. The orb for transits and natal planets varies depending on the type of aspect.

Out-of-sign aspect

An aspect where the planets are within orb of an aspect, but their respective signs do not correspond to the aspect involved. According to the Larousse Encyclopedia, the strength of the aspect is decreased.

outer planets

The planets Uranus, Neptune, and Pluto. Saturn is regarded as an outer planet by some astrologers, but I consider it to be a "bridge" planet, dividing the inner and outer planets.

paran

A paran is said to occur when two planets cross an angle (whether the same or different angles) at the same time and in the same locality. The term "paran" was coined or revived by astrologer Robert Hand.

parental angle

In natal astrology *parental angle* refers to the 4th and 10th house cusps and all planets occupying or ruling these two angular houses (which describe the parents).

Placidian house system

One of several house systems used to erect charts. The Placidus house system is used for charts consistently throughout this book.

planets

Sun: In astrology, the Sun may stand for the ego or self, and also symbolizes the father and significant males in the life.

Moon: The luminary that represents the emotional body, feelings, the nurturing or maternal instinct, early childhood, the home, the mother, and other important females.

Mercury: This planet represents the concrete mind and travel. In horary astrology, it refers to young people or adolescents.

Venus: In astrology, Venus stands for the social urge, the pleasure principle, love, affection, and beauty. Negatively, it can indicate laziness, and/or lack of will.

Mars: The planet representing the principle of physical force and energy. In a male chart, it represents passion, lust, and/or masculine assertion; negative aspects or afflictions can denote excessive force or violence. In horary astrology, Mars refers to stabbing and cutting instruments, gunshots, police, etc. A violent planet when afflicted.

Jupiter: The planet that represents the religious principle. Optimism, expansion, and growth. Negatively, it can indicate greed, self-indulgence, and irresponsibility.

Saturn: Astrologically, Saturn is the "bridge" between the inner and outer planets, and is associated with necessary limitations or frustration due to lack. It can also indicate selfishness, restriction, fears, and anxiety. Death and karma. On the positive side, it stands for discipline and responsibility. It symbolizes the father in natal astrology. In horary astrology, it refers to older or more mature persons.

Uranus: The planet that rules astrology. Associated with sudden events and impulses, freedom, independence, changes, separation, and unconventional or platonic friendships.

Neptune: In natal astrology, the planet associated with idealism, compassion, sympathy, and sacrifice. Negatively it stands for pity, feelings of persecution, deception, and a tendency to escape from reality by using drugs or alcohol. Rules disappearances.

Pluto: Represents transition from one plane to another, death, transformation. Negatively, it represents large gangs or groups, gangsters, and rape. Phobias and obsessions. A violent planet when afflicted.

Pluto

See "planets."

precession of the equinoxes

The continuous movement of the equinoxes backward through the *sidereal* zodiac as a result of the slow revolution of the Earth's axis or rotation about the ecliptic pole, at the rate of one degree every 71.5 years.

prenatal eclipse (PE)

A solar eclipse occurring just prior to birth, the sign and degree of which is marked in the natal chart. In Rose Lineman's *Your Prenatal Eclipse*, she states that when progressed or transiting aspects activate this point, people with whom we share karmic ties enter our lives and karmic situations may arise.

prenatal epoch

A rectification system in which the Moon's place approximately ten lunar months previous to birth becomes the Ascendant or Descendant at birth. Sometimes called the conception chart. Detailed rules and tables for calculating the prenatal epoch are given in E.H. Bailey's book titled *The Prenatal Epoch*.

progressed

Only *secondary* progressions are used in this book, and they are calculated on the formula that each day after birth is equal to one year of life. See "secondary progressions."

public houses

The six houses above the horizon, from the 7th house to the 12th house consecutively, and the 7th and 10th houses in particular.

qualities

Refers to the division of the twelve signs of the zodiac into three groups (of four signs each) which share common characteristics, or "qualities."

rectification

The process of adjusting a birth chart to the precise birth time when the date of birth is known, but the birth time is either unknown or inexact. Methods of rectification vary greatly, but the most common method is based on the timing of several important events in the life, and the astrologer works backwards with transits and progressions for the dates of these events to find the time of birth. In this book, we introduce the time-of-death formula for rectification; see time-of-death formula for a further explanation of this method.

retrograde

The phenomenon of a planet appearing to be traveling backward along the plane of the ecliptic from the terrestrial viewpoint .

rising

Refers to a sign or a planet which is on or near the eastern horizon, or crossing it. See "eastern horizon."

ruler

Usually refers to the planet ruling the sign on the natal Ascendant, though it can also refer to sign or house rulerships. The planet ruling the sign on the house cusp is the ruler of that house, but planets within the house also influence and modify interpretations.

Sagittarius

See "signs."

Saturn

See "planets."

Saturn/Pluto midpoint

See "midpoint."

Scorpio

See "signs."

secondary progressions

Aspects formed by planets after birth, based on a chart calculated for the same time as the natal chart but the *date* changing by one day per year of life. Used by astrologers to predict or track events after birth.

separating aspect

An aspect that has transited or progressed past the point of being exact. See "exact aspect."

semisextile

See "aspect."

semisquare

See "aspect."

sesquiquadrate

See "aspect."

sextile

See "aspect."

sign

One of the twelve divisions of the tropical zodiac. The signs follow each other thus: Aries, Taurus, Gemini, Cancer, Leo, Virgo, Libra, Scorpio, Sagittarius, Capricorn, Aquarius, Pisces. Each sign has its own distinct meaning—refer to an astrology textbook for an in-depth explanation of each sign.

soft aspect

See "aspect, modifying terms for."

solar eclipse

The phenomenon that occurs at the time of a New Moon, when the Sun and Moon form a conjunction near one of the Moon's Nodes.

South Node

See "lunar Nodes."

square

See "aspect."

stellium

Three or more planets located in one sign or house, accenting it and thus making it more important.

Sun

See "planets."

Sun/Mars midpoint

See "midpoint."

Sun/Pluto midpoint

See "midpoint."

sunrise chart

A chart calculated for the exact time of the Sun's rising at a certain location, and usually substituted for a natal chart when the true birthtime is unknown.

synastry

Comparison of two or more individual's charts to provide insight into the nature of their relationship. The astrologer examines the exchange of planetary aspects between two charts, as well as their planetary sign and house positions.

T-square

A dynamic configuration of two planets in opposition squaring a third planet which forms the base of a "T." Sometimes called a T-cross.

Taurus

See "signs."

tight aspect

See "close aspect" and "exact aspect."

time abbreviations

BST: British Summer Time
CDT: Central Daylight Time

CST: Central Standard Time
CWT: Central War Time
EDT: Eastern Daylight Time
EST: Eastern Standard Time
GMT: Greenwich Mean Time

time-of-death formula

A method of rectification based on the exchange of any one of the four angles and signs on the 1st, 4th, 7th, or 10th house cusps between the exactly timed death chart and the natal chart. It requires that the time of death be exactly known and recorded.

transit, transiting

The current position of a planet in comparison to a planet, angle, mid-point, etc. at a different time.

Transpluto

A hypothetical planet sometimes called Bacchus, as described in John Hawkins' book on Transpluto. According to Hawkins, this planet is associated with the sign of Taurus.

trine

See "aspect."

tropical zodiac

The seasonal or *moving* zodiac beginning with 0° Aries (the point of the Vernal Equinox), in contrast to the sidereal or fixed zodiac of constellations.

Uranian astrology

Sometimes loosely, but erroneously, used to refer to cosmobiology. (See "cosmobiologist.") Uranian astrology is the Hamburg school of astrology founded by Alfred Witte and Friedrich Sieggrün with an accent on delineations of midpoints.

Uranus

See "planets."

Venus

See "planets."

Vertex

Abbreviated as "Vx" in the chart. The point in the chart where the prime vertical intersects the ecliptic in the west. The antivertex is the corresponding point exactly opposite in the east. The point where the vertex falls in the chart is supposed to be the most "fated" part of the horoscope.

Violent planets

The planets Mars and Pluto are considered the most violent planets. Uranus is also sometimes indicated.

Violent signs

Aries, Libra, Scorpio, Capricorn, and Aquarius.

Virgo

See "signs."

Water signs

A triplicity of three signs: Cancer, Scorpio, and Pisces.

wide aspect

An aspect having a very wide orb. May also refer to a planet that normally might be out of orb or aspect to another planet, but is part of a T-square, grand trine, or grand square pattern, and therefore is included as part of that configuration.

Yod

Sometimes called the Finger of God or Hand of Destiny. A configuration involving three planets in which two of them form a sextile (60°), and both form an inconjunct (150°) to a third planet. It is said to indicate a strange and unusual destiny, often accompanied by disruptive changes.

Zenith

The point in the sky directly overhead which is always exactly ninety degrees in longitude from the Ascendant. It is the opposite point to the Nadir.

zodiac

A distinction should be made between the moving or tropical zodiac which is oriented in relation to the equinoxes, and the sidereal or fixed zodiac which is oriented in relation to the stars or constellations.

The tropical zodiac is divided into a 360-degree circle of twelve thirty-degree divisions of the ecliptic called signs which are used to measure the position of the planets and is the basis of the seasonal calendar. This seasonal zodiac begins with the point of the Vernal Equinox—zero degrees of the first sign, Aries—and when the Sun reaches this point on March 21 every year, it is the beginning of spring.

Bibliography

Alexander, Shana. *Very Much A Lady: The Untold Story of Jean Harris and Dr. Herman Tarnower.* Boston: Little, Brown & Co., 1983.

Baechler, Jean. *Suicides.* New York: Basic Books, 1975.

Bailey, E. H. *The Prenatal Epoch.* New York: Samuel Weiser, 1970.

Butscher, Edward. *Sylvia Plath: Method and Madness.* New York: Pocket Books, 1977.

Carpozi, George. *The Chicago Nurse Murders.* New York: Banner Books/Hearst Corp., 1967.

Carter, Charles E. O. *An Encyclopedia of Psychological Astrology.* London: Theosophical Publishing House, 1963.

_____. *The Astrology of Accidents.* London: Theosophical Publishing House, 1961.

Chalford, Ginger. *Pluto, Planet of Magic and Power.* Tempe, AZ: American Federation of Astrologers, 1984.

Connolly, Ray. *John Lennon, 1940-1980.* New York: Fontana Books, 1981.

Cooper, Paulette. *The Medical Detectives.* New York: D. Mc Kay Co., 1973.

Cunningham, Donna. *Healing Pluto Problems.* York Beach, ME: Samuel Weiser, 1986.

Darling, Harry F., M. D. and Ruth Hale Oliver. *Astro-Psychiatry.* Lakemont, GA: CSA Press, 1973.

Davies, Hunter. *The Beatles.* New York: McGraw Hill, 1985.

Davis, T. Patrick. *Sexual Assaults: Pre-Identifying Those Vulnerable.* Orlando, FL: Davis Research Reports, 1978.

Davison, R. C. *The Technique of Prediction—The New Complete System of Secondary Directing.* London: L. N. Fowler & Co., 1971.

DeVore, Nicholas. *Encyclopedia of Astrology.* New York: Philosophical Library, 1947.

Doane, Doris Chase. *Astrology—30 Years Research*. Tempe, AZ: American Federation of Astrologers, 1979.

Ebertin, Reinhold. *The Combination of Stellar Influences*. Aalen, Germany: Ebertin-Verlag, 1969.

Gauquelin, Michel. *Murderers and Psychotics*. Scientific Documents, Vol. 9. Paris, France: Laboratoire D'Etude Des Relations Entre Rythmes Cosmiques et Psychophysiologiques, 1981.

Gaute, J. H. H. and Robin Odell. *The Murderers' Who's Who*. New York: Methuen, 1979.

George, Demetra. *Mysteries of the Dark Moon: The Healing Power of the Dark Goddess*. New York: Harper Collins,1992.

Gill, Derek. *Quest—The Life of Elizabeth Kubler-Ross*. New York: Harper & Row, 1980.

Glenn, Jeannette. *The Astrological Synthesis of Female Sexual Dysfunction*. Newport Beach, CA: WSA Press, 1983.

_____. *How to Prove Astrology*. Tempe, AZ: American Federation of Astrologers, 1981.

_____. *Rectification of Unknown Birth Times*. Newport Beach, CA: WSA Press, 1984.

Goldstein-Jacobson, Ivy M. *The Dark Moon Lilith in Astrology*. Pasadena,CA: Pasadena Lithographers, 1969.

Green, Jeff. *Pluto—The Evolutionary Journey of the Soul, Vol. 1*. St. Paul, MN: Llewellyn Publications, 1986.

_____. *Uranus: Freedom from the Known*. St. Paul, MN: Llewellyn Publications, 1988.

Green, Liz. *The Astrology of Fate*. York Beach, ME: Samuel Weiser, 1984.

Guiles, Fred L. *Norma Jean: The Life of Marilyn Monroe*. New York: Simon & Schuster, 1963.

Harding, Michael. *Hymns to the Ancient Gods*. New York: Penguin Books/Arkana Series, 1992.

Harris, Jean. *Stranger in Two Worlds*. New York: Macmillan, 1986.

Haskell, Molly. *From Reverence to Rape: The Treatment of Women in the Movies*. Chicago: University of Chicago Press, 1987.

Hawkins, John Robert, M. S. *Transpluto, or Should We Call Him Bacchus?* Dallas, TX: Hawkins Enterprising Publications, 1978.

Helfer and Kempe. *The Battered Child*. Chicago: University of Chicago Press, 1987.

Hickey, Isabel M. and Bruce H. Altieri. *Pluto or Minerva*. Bridgeport, CT: Altieri Press, 1973.

Hirsch, Miriam F. *Women and Violence*. New York: Van Norstrand Reinhold Co., 1981.

Jain, Manik Chand. *Astrology in Marriage Counseling*. Lancaster, England: Pythagorean Publications, 1974.

Jones, Ann. *Women Who Kill*. New York: Holt, Rinehart & Winston, 1980.

Kendall, Elizabeth. *The Phantom Prince: My Life with Ted Bundy*. Seattle, WA: Madrona Publications, 1981.

Kimmel, Eleanora. *Patterns of Destiny, Suddenly Interrupted Lives*. Tempe, AZ: American Federation of Astrologers, 1985.

Kubler-Ross, Elizabeth. *Death and Dying*. New York: MacMillan, 1970.

Larsen, Richard W. *Bundy, The Deliberate Stranger*. New York: Pocket Books, 1986.

Leinbach, Esther V. *Degrees of the Zodiac*. Richmond, VA: Macoy Publishing Co., 1973.

Levin, Jack and James Alan Fox. *Mass Murder—America's Growing Menace*. New York: Berkley Books, 1991.

Lieber, Arnold L., M. D. *The Lunar Effect—Biological Tides and Human Emotions*. Garden City, NY: Anchor Press, Doubleday, 1978.

Lineman, Rose. *Your Prenatal Eclipse*. Tempe, AZ: American Federation of Astrologers, 1992.

Lunde, Donald T. *Murder and Madness*. Stanford, CA: Stanford Alumni Association, 1975.

March, Marion and Joan McEvers. *Astrology: Old Theme, New Thoughts*. San Diego, CA: Astro Computing Services, 1984.

Martin, Linda W. *Sylvia Plath: A Biography*. New York: Simon & Schuster, 1987.

McGinniss, Joe. *Fatal Vision*. New York: New American Library, 1983.

Michaud, Stephen S. and Hugh Aynesworth. *The Only Living Witness*. New York: Signet Books, 1983.

_____. *Ted Bundy: Conversations with a Killer*. New York: Nal/ Dutton, 1990.

Michelsen, Neil F. *The American Atlas*. San Diego, CA: Astro Computing Services, 1978.

Munkasey, Michael. *Midpoints—Unleashing the Power of the Planets*. San Diego, CA: ACS Publications, 1991.

Nash, Jay Robert. *Murder Among the Rich and Famous*. New York: Arlington House, 1983.

Norris, Joel. *Serial Killers*. New York: Anchor Books, Doubleday Dell Publishing Co., 1989.

Parker, Ann E. *Astrology and Alcoholism*. York Beach, ME: Samuel Weiser, 1982.

Penfield, Mark. *An Astrological Who's Who*. York Beach, ME: Arcane, 1972.

Rodden, Lois. *Astro Data II*. San Diego, CA: Astro Computing Services, 1980.

_____. *Astro Data III*. Tempe, AZ: American Federation of Astrologers, 1986.

_____. *Astro Data V*. Hollywood, CA: Data News Press, 1991.

_____. *Profiles of Women*. Tempe, AZ: American Federation of Astrologers, 1979.

Rowland, Edna. *How To Obtain Your Birth Certificate: With Ready-To-Use Forms*. Tempe, AZ: American Federation of Astrologers, 1990.

Rule, Ann. *Small Sacrifices—A True Story of Passion and Murder*. New York: Nal Books, 1987.

_____. *The Stranger Beside Me*. New York: Signet Books, 1980.

Savalan, Karen Ober. *Suicide, Astrology Explains Why It Happens*. Tempe, AZ: American Federation of Astrologers, 1982.

Shanks, Thomas G. *The International Atlas—World Latitudes, Longitudes and Time Changes*. San Diego, CA: Astro Computing Publications, 1985.

Slatzer, Robert F. *The Life and Curious Death of Marilyn Monroe*. Los Angeles, CA: Pinnacle Books, 1973.

Spake, Amanda. "The End of the Ride: Analyzing a Sex Crime." *Mother Jones*. April, 1980.

Speriglio, Milo. *The Marilyn Conspiracy*. New York: Simon & Schuster, 1986.

Thompson, Doris V. *Horoscope of Murder—A Study of David Berkowitz "Son of Sam."* Tempe, AZ: American Federation of Astrologers, 1980.

Tompkins, Sue. *Aspects in Astrology: A Comprehensive Guide to Interpretation*. Rockport, MA: Element Inc., 1993.

Trilling, Diana. *Mrs. Harris: The Death of the Scarsdale Diet Doctor*. New York: Harcourt Brace, 1981.

Tuton, Charlotte Ann. "Murder in Scarsdale." *American Astrology*. September, 1988.

Veatch, Robert M. *Death, Dying, and the Biological Revolution: Our Last Quest for Responsibility*. New Haven, CT: Yale University Press, 1976.

Watters, Barbara H. *The Astrologer Looks at Murder*. Washington, D.C.: Valhalla Paperbacks, 1969.

Wilson, Colin. *Written in Blood*. New York: Warner Books, 1991.

Wilson, Colin and Donald Seaman. *The Encyclopedia of Modern Murder*. New York: Arlington House, Crown Publishers, 1988.

Young, Sandra H. and Edna Rowland. *Destined for Murder*. St. Paul, MN: Llewellyn Publications, 1995.

Stay in Touch. . .

Llewellyn publishes hundreds of books on your favorite subjects

On the following pages you will find listed some books now available on related subjects. Your local bookstore stocks most of these and will stock new Llewellyn titles as they become available. We appreciate your patronage!

Order by Phone

Call toll-free within the U.S. and Canada, **1–800–THE MOON.**
In Minnesota call **(612) 291–1970.**
We accept Visa, MasterCard, and American Express.

Order by Mail

Send the full price of your order (MN residents add 7% sales tax) in U.S. funds to:

> **Llewellyn Worldwide**
> **P.O. Box 64383, Dept. L007–9**
> **St. Paul, MN 55164–0383, U.S.A.**

Postage and Handling

- $4.00 for orders $15.00 and under
- $5.00 for orders over $15.00
- No charge for orders over $100.00

We ship UPS in the continental United States. We cannot ship to P.O. boxes. Orders shipped to Alaska, Hawaii, Canada, Mexico, and Puerto Rico will be sent first-class mail.

International orders: Airmail—add freight equal to price of each book to the total price of order, plus $5.00 for each non-book item (audiotapes, etc.). Surface mail—Add $1.00 per item.

Allow 4–6 weeks delivery on all orders. Postage and handling rates subject to change.

Group Discounts

We offer a 20% quantity discount to group leaders or agents. You must order a minimum of 5 copies of the same book to get our special quantity price.

Free Catalog

Get a free copy of our color catalog, *New Worlds of Mind and Spirit.* Subscribe for just $10.00 in the United States and Canada ($20.00 overseas, first class mail). Many bookstores carry *New Worlds*—ask for it!

DESTINED FOR MURDER
Profiles of Six Serial Killers with Astrological Commentary
Sandra Harrisson Young & Edna Rowland
This is not just another book about serial killers. *Destined for Murder* addresses the question, "why did they do it?" Was it an aberration in their personalities or was it their astrological destinies? Read the personal stories of Ed Gein, Jeffrey Dahmer and five other madmen. Is it possible that they had an astrological "blueprint" for murder? Had their birth charts been cast in childhood, could they have been directed toward a different path in life?

The book is arranged for easy reading. In the first part of each chapter, master story-teller Sandra Harrisson Young weaves the tale of each killer: his childhood and family, the murders he committed and his eventual capture. The remaining half of the chapter is handed over to professional astrologer Edna Rowland, who follows the pivotal points in the killer's life as they're actually happening and discovers whether or not these pivotal points were astrologically pre-ordained. The results, you will find, are astounding.
ISBN: 1-56718-832-X, 224 pgs., 6 x 9, softcover
$12.95

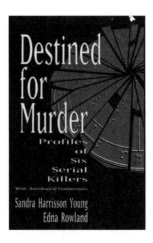

ASTROLOGY OF THE FAMED
Startling Insights Into Their Lives
Noel Tyl

The lives of Cleopatra, Dracula, St. Francis of Assisi, Beethoven and Leonardo da Vinci take on exciting new dimensions in this work by master astrologer Noel Tyl. History buffs and astrologers alike will be amazed at how he merges the technique of rectification with the adventure, genius and drama of five of the most unique and provocative lives in all of history.

Astrologers use rectification when they don't know someone's birth date; they work backward and allow life events to determine the time of birth. To determine the birth month of Cleopatra, for example, Tyl transplanted himself back to 69 B.C. and walked through her footsteps to translate her actions into a horoscope that symbolizes her life's events and her character.

And there is so much more to this book than rectifications. There is good solid history and analysis of the personalties. Tyl then uses astrology to color in their motivations and mind-sets over the black-on-white historical facts.
1-56718-735-8, 384 pp., 6 x 9, softcover
$19.95

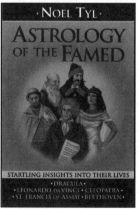

VISIONS OF MURDER
A Novel by Florence Wagner McClain
Set in a scenic Oregon resort town surrounded by moun-
tains and vast natural beauty, this suspense novel delves
into the real problems of New Mexico's black market of
stolen Indian artifacts. *Visions of Murder* mixes fact-based
psychic experiences with lively archeological dialogue in
a plot that unravels the high toll this black market exacts
in lives, knowledge, and money.

David Manning was gunned down in an execution-style
shooting outside his office. Unknown to his wife Janet,
David had just discovered evidence in his employer's
data bank of money-laundering connected to a black market in Indian artifacts.

Janet embarks on a personally exhaustive investigation
into the death of her husband when she unearths a kind
of dirt she's not used to handling. Elements of the occult,
romance, and murder simmer hotly in this bubbling caul-
dron of mystery that is as informative as it is absorbing.

**1-56718-452-9, 336 pgs., mass market, illus., softcover
$5.99**

YOUR PLANETARY PERSONALITY
Everything You Need to Make Sense of Your Horoscope

Dennis Oakland

This book deepens the study of astrological interpretation for professional and beginning astrologers alike. Dennis Oakland's interpretations of the planets in the houses and signs are the result of years of study of psychology, sciences, symbolism, Eastern philosophy plus the study of birth charts from a psychotherapy group. Unlike the interpretations in other books, these emphasize the life processes involved and facilitate a greater understanding of the chart. Includes 100-year ephemeris.

Even if you now know *nothing* about astrology, Dennis Oakland's clear instructions will teach you how to construct a complete and accurate birth chart for anyone born between 1900 to 1999. After you have built your chart, he will lead you through the steps of reading it, giving you indepth interpretations of each of your planets. When done, you will have the satisfaction that comes from increased self-awareness *and* from being your *own* astrologer!

This book is also an excellent exploration for psychologists and psychiatrists who use astrology in their practices.

0-87542-594-1, 580 pp., 7 x 10, softcover
$24.95

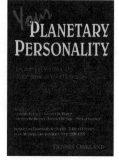

ASTROLOGY AND THE GAMES PEOPLE PLAY
A Tool for Self-Understanding in Work & Relationships

Spencer Grendahl

Expand your self-awareness and facilitate personal growth with the Astro-analysis approach to astrology! Astro-analysis is a completely new and unique system that enables you to combine simple astrological information with the three-ring model of basic ego states—Parent, Adult and Child—used in popular psychology. This easy-to-follow technique makes available to the average person psychological insights that are generally available only to astrologers. Not only is it easy to transcribe your horoscope onto Astro-analysis' three-sphere diagram, but you will find that this symbolic picture provides accurate and meaningful perceptions into the energy patterns of your personality, clearly delineating the areas that may be "overweighted" or most in need of balance. This material is enhanced by examples and explanations of horoscopes of actual people.

Astro-analysis is a powerful self-help tool that will quickly make you aware of the basis for your behavior patterns and attitudes, so you can get a new perspective on your relationships with others and determine the most promising strategies for personal growth.

1-56718-338-7, 224 pp., 7 x 10, softcover
$12.95